*"I wholeheartedly affirm this reformation in the contemporary prophetic movement and for the raising up a new breed of Jesus-centered prophets who are grounded in the Word, who love intimacy with God more than ministry to people, who preach and live holiness, who renounce carnal prosperity, and who speak of the Lord's goodness as well as His severity. If this book offends you, then it is probably the very thing you need!"*

−**Dr. Michael L. Brown**, President, FIRE School of Ministry

*"Jeremiah has done a great service to the next generation in writing this book. With fearless honesty and fatherly tenderness he addresses the key pitfalls of the prophetic movement while soundly setting the prophetic ministry in its most vibrant place – intimacy with Jesus, the revelation of God's character and nature, the whole counsel of God's Word, fervent intercession, and humble, loving service to the Body. Oh, may the new prophetic generation arise. Both the need and opportunity have never been so great!"*

**–Allen Hood,** Associate Director, IHOPKC and President, International House of Prayer University

*"This book is a clarion call to the prophetic movement to come into a new place of intimacy and friendship with the Holy Spirit, feeding on the nature and character of God, and being given to the place of intercession. It's*

*these components that will bring forth a new prophetic generation in the earth. In "I see A New Prophetic Generation" Jeremiah Johnson lays out with profound clarity what God is doing in the prophetic movement right now. Jeremiah is a dear friend, and a trusted prophetic voice. The message of this book doesn't come from a "shotgun prophet" that's releasing rebukes, but comes from a broken, weeping, praying and prophetic shepherd that is calling us as messengers back to the heart of the true prophetic."*

—**Corey Russell,** serves on the senior leadership team at IHOPKC, Instructor, International House of Prayer University

# I See
# A New
# Prophetic
# Generation

**Jeremiah Johnson**

Cover design by Darin Shiflett
www.lifedesignsandmedia.com

To order copies of this book and other products from
Jeremiah Johnson in bulk quantities, please contact us at:
www.jeremiahjohnson.tv

# DEDICATION

To the New Prophetic Generation…

May the Father grant us His grace to honor the prophetic

generations that have gone before us and the courage to

lead the ones coming behind us

# CONTENTS

# ACKNOWLEDGMENTS

I would like to thank my earthly father Joseph Johnson for the sacrifice he made to raise me in an environment that fostered the prophetic ministry in my life from a very early age. Thanks for constantly encouraging me to never despise my youth and believing that God really was speaking through me, even at nine years old!

A special thank you to Christopher Johnson and Barry Nichols who have spiritually fathered me for many years now. Each one of you have been used as an instrument in the hand of the Father to faithfully challenge and exhort me over and over again. Your love for the Word of God and the preeminence of Jesus Christ in all things has radically impacted my life and I love you both for it!

Thanks to the community of believers at Heart of the

Father Ministry for embracing the corporate prophetic call upon my life and receiving the words and heart of the Father with grace and open hearts time and time again.

To my dearly beloved wife Morgan and two children Bella and Israel, thanks for your constant affection and love for me as a father and husband. Thanks for releasing and praying for me as I travel around the world and impart the portion of grace the Father has given me to His body. I am forever indebted to you for your countless sacrifices. I love you with my whole heart.

Lastly, thanks to the Father, Son, and Holy Spirit! You all work so well together! Father, thank you for your great heart! Jesus, thank you for your leadership! Holy Spirit, thanks for being my best friend! May this book bring you much glory, honor, and praise

# FOREWORD

As an older minister in the Lord, I have the advantage of having lived through several moves of the Spirit, including the prophetic. I've seen and been part of both the good and the bad, the holy and the misfocused. I know firsthand many of the benefits and abuses, the glory and the garbage, and have witnessed the fruit of both truth and error. I've personally known some who ministered out of ambition and have had the privilege of knowing others who did so from a genuine heart for God and for His people. I've grieved over those who began well, but finished badly, because they failed to deal adequately with broken areas of character. *"Pursue... the sanctification without which no one will see the Lord"* (Hebrews 12:14).

In renewal circles we have long been obsessed with anointing, and have too often fallen down to worship at the altar of signs and wonders, supernatural experiences, and self-oriented teachings that claim to make us healthy, wealthy, and wise. We've idolized those who could provide us with experiences of these things, or the appearance of them. We've done all this at the expense of a focus on character and we have paid a high price for it in destruction and in wounded saints. Often we've seen the gospel we preach discredited in the eyes of the world as a result.

Many times I've said and written that God doesn't care one bit for anointing. He can anoint a donkey, and in the case of Balaam's ass, He did. He cares for people and that means He cares for character formation, that we might conform to the image of the Son (Romans 8:29).

Having observed and personally experienced His dealings over a lifetime, I know that, given a choice, when no other option seems open, He will sacrifice the anointing and destroy a ministry in order to save the man who leads it. He can raise up anointing by a mere breath or a wave of His hand, but a man or a woman is a thing most precious to Him. For men and women He gave His life, His only Son. Next to that, the anointing that might be here today and fade tomorrow pales to insignificance.

Over the years in word and in print I've stated that if we focus on being supernatural, we will end up in shipwreck, but that if we focus on intimacy with the Father through Jesus, we will end up being supernatural. True prophetic people, as well as real disciples in any positions of leadership, choose to seek intimacy with our Lord, not in order to produce supernatural displays and experiences, but in order to be transformed into the image of the One who gave all to unite us with Himself. In Jesus' earthly ministry, people recognized His disciples as those who had been with Him. Their intimacy with Him changed them and, from that change - forged in intimacy - flowed their authority.

I have long prophesied that a change of leadership in the body of Christ is coming. I have spoken of an old guard giving way to a new generation of leaders who have been trained in hiddenness, in brokenness of heart and spirit, toward a shaping of character that renders them safe to wield the power and word of God. I have prayed that I myself am not too old to be included in that number. Jeremiah Johnson points to, and is part of, that new generation of leaders and prophetic voices whose goal and hunger is conformity to the image of the Son.

He issues a clear and resounding cry for integrity in prophetic ministry, based in the nature and character of God imprinted into His servants.

Do not, therefore, read this book expecting to be amazed by stories of the supernatural. Read it as a guide and exhortation to move toward the only goal that ultimately matters. What are we becoming? If God is love, as the apostle John so firmly taught, then we couldn't possibly hunger after anything more vital than becoming as He is in every aspect of who we are.

−**R. Loren Sandford**, Senior Pastor at New Song Church and Ministries, Denver, Colorado. Author of "Purifying the Prophetic: Breaking Free from the Spirit of Self-focus", "Understanding Prophetic People: Blessings and Problems with the Prophetic Gift", and "The Prophetic Church: Wielding the Power to Change the World".

# INTRODUCTION

"You were born to write this book." These were the words that the Holy Spirit spoke to me as I sat down to write what you are about to read. My mother was only a few months pregnant with me when she had a dream and the Lord told her to name me Jeremiah. He said that I was to be a prophet to the nations, but more specifically, my life would mirror the call on Jeremiah the prophet's life as mentioned in Jeremiah 1:10 when God says, *"See I have appointed you this day over the nations and over kingdoms to uproot and tear down, to destroy and overthrow, to build and to plant."*

Make no mistake, the book that you have in your hands will seek to uproot and tear down strongholds and lies in the prophetic movement that have existed for years. The following pages will attempt to destroy and overthrow mindsets and practices that are not built upon the foundation of the Word of God and therefore distort His Character and Nature. More than any other pursuit, this work is dedicated to building and planting a new foundation in the prophetic movement that will foster and give birth to a new prophetic generation that the body of Christ has never seen before.

I realize that by using the terminology " a new prophetic generation," that some will believe I am disrespecting and trampling upon the "former prophetic generations." On the contrary, I have the utmost respect and honor for the prophetic generations that have gone before us and paid such a heavy price for what much of the prophetic movement now walks in. I am forever indebted to numerous prophetic fathers who poured into my life as early as nine years old and recognized the call that God had placed upon my life.

It is because of the heavy price that has been paid and because of where I believe God the Father desires to take the prophetic movement that I have been so burdened to write this book.

Paul said in 1 Corinthians 13:11, *"When I was a child, I spoke like a child, I thought like a child, I reasoned like a child; when I became a man, I did away with childish things."*

The prophetic movement is no longer a child. What we could give excuse for and plead ignorance about in the 1960's and 70's, we will now in the 21st century have to give an account for. The following pages are a call to maturity. The heart of the Father is asking the prophetic movement to put childish mindsets and practices behind us and start taking responsibility for our mistakes and more importantly repenting where we have gone wrong. We are far enough along in the prophetic movement to stop making excuses for our immaturity and start erecting a standard of righteousness that sets itself upon the very desires of God for our lives as a new prophetic generation since the beginning of time.

The greatest days of the prophetic movement are right around the corner, but without a call to repentance among prophetic voices and a challenge to maturity and putting childish ways behind us, we will never see such days. In fact, without the intervention of God Himself in the prophetic movement, I'm deeply afraid that we are headed for disaster.

I have not written what you are about to read from a platform with my finger pointed down at anyone, but rather as a broken hearted young man down on my knees, crying out to prophets and prophetic people alike, asking that we would hear the voice of the Father as He says, "Come let us reason together." I cannot and will not let my fears of being labeled as judgmental and critical keep me from releasing this tremendous burden any longer. My personal prayer for you as you read this book is that you might *"hear the truth spoken in love, that we might grow up into ALL ASPECTS into Him, who is the head, Jesus Christ."* (Ephesians 4:15) This is a call to intimacy. This is a call to return to the devotion of our youth. This is a cry from the heart of the Father to the prophetic movement: It's time to grow up and put childish and immature ways behind us. Let the healing begin!

# - 1 -
# POLLUTED WELLS

On October 15, 2013, I had a dream where I found myself walking through a forest with thousands of prophets, and as we came to an opening in the forest, a large lake appeared in front of us. Now, the journey through the forest had taken many days, and a number of the prophets were exhausted and dying of thirst.

As the prophets saw the lake appear before them, many went into a full sprint without looking into the water. I found it interesting that many of those running to the water were older, seasoned prophets that I recognized. As I watched them run, I suddenly looked at the water in the lake, and to my horror, it was polluted and contaminated with all sorts of waste and trash.

I noticed that while all the prophets were very thirsty, only a few recognized that the water was not healthy and not from the Spirit of God. I began to weep in the dream and said to the Father, "What is wrong with these prophets? Are they blind? They have become like Esau who out of his exhaustion traded his birthright for a bowl of soup."

The Father responded back to me in the dream and said, "Jeremiah, many prophets in America are drinking from polluted and contaminated waters because they are tired and weary. They are prophesying out of the flesh and exchanging the pure word of My Spirit for meaningless chatter that stirs up the people. They are mere false alarms."

As God continued to speak to me in the dream, I suddenly woke up and sat up in my bed. The Holy Spirit immediately spoke to me from Deuteronomy 29:29, which says, *"The secret things belong to the Lord our God, but the things revealed belong to us and to our sons forever, that we may observe all the words of this law."*

I said to the Holy Spirit, "What are you trying to tell me through this verse?" He said, "You prophets believe that maturity looks like having a word for every event, but I say that maturity looks like not having to have a word for every event, unless I give you one. Do you not know that many prophets in the earth are simply prophesying from the flesh because they are upset that I have not said anything to them concerning the state of America? It is merely their pride and desire to be seen and heard that causes them to operate in anger and prophesy. Let it not be so with you!"

I believe with all my heart that we are living in the greatest days that the body of Christ has ever seen and known. As I continue to travel around America and the nations of the earth ministering at revival services, prophetic conferences, and shepherding the flock that God has given me in Lakeland, FL, my heart is continually encouraged by many in the body of Christ who are hungry to give the Lamb of God the full reward of His suffering, and to receive everything in their life that His death, burial, and resurrection paid for. I am constantly filled with hope, comfort, and strength by many of the wonderful things that I see happening in the body.

## The Burden Released

With all that being said, I have also received a very specific burden from the Father for prophets and the prophetic movement. Over the years as I have continued to train and equip thousands of prophetic people in my prophetic school, traveled across the country speaking at prophetic conferences, and shepherding people prophetically in a local church, the burden has increased as I have recognized that we are currently witnessing a simple yet profound crisis in the prophetic movement. I am continuing to see dangerous patterns among prophetic voices and blatant blindness toward foundational issues that if not addressed, will cripple the movement and ultimately cause a total disregard for the need for it.

The crisis to which I am referring was addressed (in part) in the dream that you just read. In essence, I believe that many of the prophets (and in turn the prophetic movement in America) have begun to drink from contaminated and polluted wells because they are tired and weary. Why are so many exhausted you ask? The unfortunate and simple answer is recorded in Jeremiah 23:18 as God asks, *"But who has stood in the council of the Lord, that he should see and hear His word? Who has given heed to His word and listened?"*

**I Miss You**

If ever there was a prophetic word that was necessary to give to the prophets of God in the earth right now, it would simply be, "I miss you," says your Father. To the Father's heartbreak and dismay, many of the prophetic voices in the earth are choosing to prophesy out of their gifting, rather than prophesying from time spent with Him. I believe that we are going to see a standard raised up in the prophetic movement in the years to come where the new prophetic generation will actually refuse to prophesy unless they have prayed and spent time with their Father in heaven. They will not rely on their gifting, but rely on intimate time spent in the secret place.

The issue that I am addressing is not a new one nor is it cherished by many, but I believe with all my heart that the contaminated and polluted wells that the prophetic voices are drinking from in this hour are not only damaging the body of Christ, but most devastating of all, it is blaspheming the testimony of Jesus in the earth!

Because of the lack of time spent with God, many messengers are striving, self-promoting, and trading their birthright (intimacy with God) for a bowl of soup (entertaining people)! We are exchanging the pure word of the Lord for diluted and watered down messages that cater to the flesh.

Not only that, but because we are not spending time with God and receiving His instructions and assignments, many are prophesying outside the bounds of their jurisdiction. They are like the prophets Jeremiah prophesied about in chapter 23:21, when God said, *"I did not send these prophets but they ran. I did not speak to them but they prophesied."* The reason why these prophets ran and he did not send them and why they prophesied when He did not speak is because they were persuaded and allured by the demands and carnal desires of the people, rather than waiting on God for His words and His answers. In the next verse Jeremiah says again, *"But if they had of stood in My council, they would have announced My words to My people, and would have turned them back from the evil of their deeds."*

## The Clarion Call

I would humbly like to issue a clarion call to the prophetic movement in America to return to the council of the Lord and refuse to prophesy unless we have prayed, fasted, and sought His face. While so many are simply prophesying from their gifting, God is raising up a new prophetic generation led by a new breed of prophets who will prophesy from the deepest recesses of

His Heart and release a spirit of revelation to the body of Christ that is simply not available to those who do not know how to travail in the secret place.

I want to be very clear, the exponential rise of inaccurate prophecy in the prophetic movement, the impurity and total disregard for holiness among the messengers, and the lack of keen eyesight and clarity that the body of Christ so desperately needs in this hour is the direct result of prophetic voices not spending time in intimacy with the Father and giving themselves to understanding His character and nature.

Revelation 19:10 states, *"the spirit of prophecy is the testimony of Jesus."* In other words, who we as prophetic messengers say that God is will directly affect the way we prophesy." With so little time spent with God these days and more of a desire among prophets and prophetic people to minister to the saints rather than to minister to the Lord, we can expect a total misrepresentation of the heart of God to His people.

# - 2 -
# THE CHARACTER AND NATURE OF GOD

God the Father is raising up a new breed of prophets who will lead a new prophetic generation in the earth that are going to spend the majority of their lives ministering to Him, rather than ministering to people. Over the years, I have found that a secret to walking in the fresh anointing of the Holy Spirit is to actually take the anointing that He releases to us as His servants and minister it back to Him. It is then out of this intimate relationship that He begins to move upon His people as we minister.

## Impartation and Activation

There is an unhealthy emphasis and priority being placed on impartation and activation in the prophetic movement that is giving breed to a generation of those like "Simon, the Sorcerer," masquerading around as prophets of God. So many are using and being taught soulish means to obtain the power of God, and are actually being encouraged to do so by leaders! I am currently witnessing thousands of young adults attending supernatural lifestyle and prophetic schools where they have prophets and leaders lay hands on them, activate them, and send them out on the streets and these individuals do not know the character and nature of God nor have they been taught its importance.

While I believe the Father's heart is broken over this current trend, I foresee days ahead in the body of Christ where a new breed of prophets leading a new prophetic generation is going to come forth in the earth who are saturated with the character and nature of God. These men and women will see their primary calling in life to be filled with the knowledge of God. Their focus will not be on the applause of men, but on the deep and overwhelming affirmation of God their Father. They will not spend their time asking the Father for His words, but rather seek to connect to His Heart. They have realized over the years that if they have His heart, then they will have His words!

We must spend less and less time trying to explain prophecy to people and laying hands on them to receive our "gift," and more and more time teaching people about the character and nature of God. When the word "prophetic ministry" is spoken, I would like you to immediately associate it with who God is. The true foundation of everything truly "prophetic" is the Character and Nature of God. If we do not know God through spending time with Him, then our footing from which we prophesy to people will be unbalanced, dangerous, and at times heretical.

We must have a Biblical understanding of the character and nature of God in order to properly reveal His heart and speak His words to His people. Who God is as revealed in the Scriptures and in Jesus Christ must surpass our own experience of Him on a personal level.

## The Character and Nature of God

One of the greatest mistakes we can make in the prophetic movement is to limit our revelation of who God is based on our personal experiences alone, and not according to the full council of God as revealed in the Bible. For example, some prophetic people have had deep personal encounters with the goodness and kindness of God, but from their experience and therefore erroneously, they portray God as if He is ONLY good and kind. They categorically reject any idea of the correction, discipline and rebuke of the Lord because that has not been their personal experience. I want to reiterate one more time: Who we say Jesus is will directly affect the way we prophesy.

The source of all prophetic inaccuracy is not only found in not spending time with God in intimacy, but failing to embrace every aspect of His character and nature. To embrace aspects of His Nature such as His goodness and kindness and to reject others such as His truth, justice, and righteousness will surely lead us down the path of inaccurate prophecy and even worse, to misrepresent the heart of God to His people. It is a serious mistake to spend our lives simply prophesying and limiting God to two aspects of His Character and Nature and fail to release the many other aspects of who He is that people so desperately need imparted to their life.

I believe many of the prophetic words that God wants to release over His people in this hour have nothing to do with what we are going to receive, and everything to do with who we are becoming. We are going to witness a rise in prophetic words that are directly geared toward assisting people in partnering with their ultimate call in life: *"To be transformed and conformed to the image of His Son"* (Romans 8:29).

Imagine the aspects of God's character and nature like arrows in a quiver. What we are witnessing today is many prophetic voices who only have one or two arrows in their quiver. In essence, that's who God is to them and every person that they prophesy to is only going to get one or two of those aspects.

Unless we wholeheartedly give ourselves as prophetic people to embracing every aspect of the Father's character and nature as revealed in Scripture (and even those that stretch beyond our personal experience), we will not only limit Him but also misrepresent Him to people! This is the greatest disservice we can do to God as His messengers! We have to allow Him to work every part of Himself inside of us or we will not communicate or portray Him to His people in a way that is in alignment with the Scriptures.

## The Word of God

I would now like to look deeply and intently into the Scriptures to discover the character and nature of God. I must briefly note however, how little emphasis is being placed on the written Word of God among prophets and the prophetic movement. I cannot count how many prophetic conferences where I have personally spoken where pulling out my Bible and preaching from the Word of God was seen as a bad omen among prophetic people. I have had multiple pastors and people on many different occasions tell me, "Put down your Bible and prophesy to us."

The divorce that I'm seeing from the Word of God and the movement of the Holy Spirit as I travel is producing a generation of prophetic people that are hungry to be stimulated with words of blessing, but who do not want to get impregnated with the truth of God's Word. So many prophetic people want to be tickled with promises of destiny and wealth, rather than be provoked into holiness and righteousness.

God the Father is raising up a new breed of prophets in the earth that are going to teach and encourage a new prophetic generation to primarily give themselves to the study of His revealed will through the Scriptures, and less time chasing after His hidden will through strange and oftentimes bizarre experiences. I see such incredible standards being raised up in the days ahead at prophetic schools, that prophetic people will not be allowed to prophesy unless they can accurately back up what they are claiming God said with a Scripture, and specifically not use it out of context.

We desperately need to see the Word of God handled accurately and with integrity in the prophetic movement. God is raising up a new prophetic generation that will stop searching the Scriptures to justify their prophetic experiences and start using the Word of God as the foundation and litmus test to see whether their so-called prophetic experiences are even biblical.

## The New Breed

I see days ahead in the prophetic movement where people are going to become so tired of the counterfeit, so fed up with hearing about another angelic visitation or out of body experience, and begin to cry out for fresh voices that have a genuine revelation of the God-Man Jesus Christ!

This new prophetic generation coming forth in the earth will give themselves to the preeminence of Jesus Christ, rather than a pursuit of gold dust, feathers, and gemstones. They will be welcomed with open arms by numerous pastors and leaders all over America who are hungry to see and hear true voices from above. These sons and daughters will live and minister from the Throne Room, rather than prostitute their gifts in a showroom called "church".

I prophesy to you: Be on the lookout for one of the

greatest blessings and waves of encouragement that the body of Christ has ever known: a new breed of prophets leading a new prophetic generation who are radically Jesus centered and who love the Word of God more than they love their own experiences.

## The Radiance

Let's dive into the Scriptures as we discover who God is. Hebrews 1:1-3 says, "God, after He spoke long ago to the fathers in the prophets in many portions and in many ways, in these last days he has spoken to us in His Son, whom He appointed heir of all things, through whom also He made the world. And He is the radiance of His glory and the exact representation of His nature, and upholds all things by the word of His power. When He had made purification of sins, He sat down at the right hand of the Majesty on high."

I want to specifically look at verse three where it says, "He (Jesus) is the radiance of His (the Father) glory." The Greek word for radiance is: apaugasma, which means, "an out-raying or a shining forth." Jesus was the radiance of the Father's Glory. In other words, Jesus Christ came to planet earth to give expression to His Father's Glory. Jesus could have said, "If you want to know what My Father's Glory is all about, look at Me!"

John the Beloved echoed this is John 1:14 when He said, *"And the Word (Christ) became flesh (human, incarnate) and tabernacled (fixed His tent of flesh, lived awhile) among us; and we [actually] saw His glory (His honor, His majesty), such glory as an only begotten son receives from his father, full of grace (favor, loving-kindness) and truth."* (AMP)

## Show Me Your Glory

John and the disciples beheld the glory of the Father revealed in Jesus Christ His Son. The question has to be asked then, what is the glory of God? Some describe the glory of God as His anointing. When people fall down or laugh or cry etc., many say, "Now that's the glory." Others say the glory of God is found in His presence. They say, "It's that 'feeling!" While all these ideas point to exterior and outward manifestations, I would like to make a case that according to the Scriptures, the Glory of God is the character and nature of God. The Glory of God is who He is in His Person. Jesus Christ, the Son of God came to the earth to put on display and carried in Himself every aspect of His Father's character and nature.

In Exodus 33:12-16 it says,

*"Then Moses said to the Lord, "See, You say to me, 'Bring up this people!' But You Yourself have not let me know whom You will send with me. Moreover, You have said, 'I have known you by name, and you have also found favor in My sight.' Now therefore, I pray You, if I have found favor in Your sight, let me know Your ways that I may know You, so that I may find favor in Your sight. Consider too, that this nation is Your people."* And He said, *"My presence shall go with you, and I will give you rest. Then he said to Him, "If Your presence does not go with us, do not lead us up from here. For how then can it be known that I have found favor in Your sight, I and Your people? Is it not by Your going with us, so*

*that we, I and Your people, may be distinguished from all the other people who are upon the face of the earth?"*

Moses has found himself in a desperate season. God has asked Him to lead the people into their destiny and He is telling God that he cannot go any further unless the presence of God accompanies them.

In 33:17 God responds back and says, *"'I will also do this thing of which you have spoken; for you have found favor in My sight and I have known you by name.' Then Moses said, 'I pray You, show me Your glory!'"*

As soon as God promises to send His presence with Moses and the people, Moses asks, perhaps, the most interesting question in all of the Scriptures! Imagine getting to ask God one question while you are up on a mountain about to lead a nation into their destiny. What would you ask for? His protection? His provision? His guidance?

Moses asks God to, "Show me your glory!" And how does God respond? Verse 17 says,

> *"'I Myself will make all My Goodness pass before you, and will proclaim the name of the LORD before you; and I will be gracious to whom I will be gracious, and will show compassion on whom I will show compassion.' But He said, 'You cannot see My face, for no man can see Me and live!' Then the Lord said, 'Behold, there is a place by Me, and you shall stand there on the rock; and it will come about, while My glory is passing by, that I will put you in the cleft of the rock and cover you with My hand until I have passed by. Then I will take My*

*hand away and you shall see My back, but*

*My face shall not be seen.'"*

In essence, God says in response to Moses's question to see His glory, "Okay Moses, I will show you who I am, but I have to hide you behind a rock or my glory with destroy you!"

So Moses gets behind the rock and in chapter 34:5-9 God reveals His Character and Nature to Moses as the Scriptures say,

> *"The LORD descended in the cloud and*
> *stood there with him as he called upon the*
> *name of the LORD. Then the LORD passed*
> *by in front of him and proclaimed, 'The*
> *LORD, the LORD God, compassionate and*
> *gracious, slow to anger, and abounding in*
> *loving kindness and truth; who keeps loving*

*kindness for thousands, who forgives iniquity, transgression and sin; yet He will by no means leave the guilty unpunished, visiting the iniquity of fathers on the children and on the grandchildren to the third and fourth generations.'"*

Incidentally, when the LORD said, *"I Myself will make all My Goodness pass before you,"* the Hebrew word for "before" may also be translated "through" you. Therefore, as the LORD passed "before Moses" with the qualities of His Goodness and Glory, He also caused all of those qualities "to pass through Moses" so that Moses could know Him **experientially** in His character and nature. We must understand that the primary purpose of God revealing His glory to us is to bring inward character transformation. (2 Corinthians 3:18)

Ponder being up on top of a mountain needing to hear

from God. You are carrying an incredible burden from the many people that you are leading and you are desperate for God's blessing and direction. It seems best to have a prophetic meeting with God on top of the mountain in hopes that He gives you clarity and precise instructions so you ask Him to show you His glory. To your great surprise, God does not show you your future and neither did He with Moses. He simply reveals Himself to you and says, "What you need to carry out the destiny that I have placed upon your life is a revelation of my character and nature. It is knowing Me that will secure your future."

I believe that just as Moses had an encounter with the Glory of God on Mt. Sinai in a most desperate season, so the body of Christ is about to experience God in ways not seen before. Let it be known though, to the surprise of many, that the new prophetic generation being revealed in the earth, will not primarily prophesy to desperate people and leaders about their future. This new prophetic generation is going to prophesy to people about the character and nature of God because they understand just as Moses found, that what people need in order to fulfill their destiny is not more words of false hope and prosperity, but a revelation of the character and nature of God. Just as God revealed Himself to Moses and knew that's exactly what He needed to lead the people, so is God the Father releasing a new prophetic generation led by a new breed of prophets to the body of Christ that are going to primarily reveal and teach on who God is to the people. That, in and of itself, will be more of a blessing and protection than any other so-called prophetic word that they could ever deliver.

## When God Reveals Himself

It would be foolishness to move on to another subject without properly looking more intently into how God is revealing Himself to Moses in Exodus 34. From what I see, there are seven major aspects of God's character and nature that He has chosen to reveal to Moses in this incredible moment in history. Man has chosen throughout the centuries to declare who they believe God is to the masses. But let us pay close attention when it is God Himself who has chosen to reveal who He Is! It therefore beckons us as New Covenant believers to study these aspects more closely that we might fully know our Lord and Savior Jesus Christ, who according to Hebrews 1:3 and the testimony of John the Beloved in John 1:14 came to be the out-raying and shining forth of this glory that we now look at and give ourselves to study.

## His Glory Equals His Goodness

The most important part of this self-revelation by Yahweh, the LORD, is that He equates His glory with His goodness! His glory is His goodness! Or to put it another way: HIS GLORY = HIS GOODNESS! The goodness of His Person, and all the various qualities and meanings of His goodness constitute(s) His glory. Strong's Concordance defines the Hebrew word for "goodness" as, "to be good in the widest sense, to be better, to be cheerful, to be well: beautiful, best, better, bountiful, favor, gladness, gracious, joyful, loving, merry, pleasure, precious, sweet, wealth, welfare, beauty." The Theological Wordbook of the Old Testament (pg. 793) gives these meanings to the Hebrew word: "Good, Pleasant, Beautiful, Delightful, Glad, Joyful, Correct (Correctness) and Right (Rightness)."

All of these qualities constitute His goodness, which is His Glory! But Yahweh, the LORD God, goes on to further define His glory and goodness to Moses, and explain to him the Attributes of His character and nature through which He relates to mankind. What God said looks like the following.

**MY GLORY = MY GOODNESS (AS EXPRESSED IN):**

**My Graciousness**

**My Compassion/Mercy**

**My Longsuffering**

**My Loving-kindness**

**My Truthfulness = Trustworthiness/Faithfulness**

**My Forgiveness**

## My Justness = Justice

It is vitally important to note the last two meanings from the Hebrew Theological Wordbook mentioned above: correctness and rightness. These two constitute His justness, as explained by the LORD as: *"...yet He will by no means leave the guilty unpunished, visiting the iniquity of the fathers on the children and on the grandchildren, to the third and fourth generations."* There are many today who have missed or ignored this last statement by the LORD, and have eliminated it from their thinking. We cannot ignore what He has said concerning Himself! His justness, His correctness and rightness are parts of his goodness! When God chooses to bring correction to our lives and make our crooked ways right, it is a demonstration of His goodness and not a form of punishment as many believe.

God chose to reveal Himself to Moses as good because He knew Moses needed to know that He was serving a Creator, Maker, and Father that had his and the peoples' best interest in mind. He only had righteous and holy plans toward them and their future.

I love it when God chooses to release His goodness upon His people, whether it is through a prophetic word or an act of kindness on His part. God has been unusually good and kind toward me over many years and I constantly rely on His goodness toward me for every step of my journey.

## His Goodness in Redding

A few years ago I took a trip with several others to Redding, California, because we wanted to see what God was doing at Bethel Church, led by Bill Johnson. After we arrived and spent some time at several of their services, we ended up in their prayer room on a Saturday morning. We sat in the prayer room for several hours as we prayed and soaked in God's Presence, and when we were ready to head to lunch, a man and his family caught my attention. God immediately spoke to me about this man and the call on his life. I sensed that God the Father wanted to affirm to him His good heart toward this man. Little did I know that I was about to have an encounter like few that I have had since!

I walked up to the man and shared the small vision God had given me and reminded him of God's goodness, that He had his and his family's best interest in mind and the man fell out of his seat and began to weep. Not expecting this reaction, I took a step back while his wife and daughters got on the floor and surrounded him in prayer. I decided after several minutes to leave and head to lunch. As we got into the car, the voice of the Holy

Spirit said to me, "Invite that man and his family to lunch. My goodness has only just begun." I knew in that moment that something very unique was about to take place that day.

So I went back into the prayer room and asked the man's wife if they would like to go to lunch with us. In shock, she responded, "Yes," in a foreign accent. She spoke in a language that I did not know to her family and they all were instantly filled with joy. They followed us to a restaurant and we sat at the table with them and their three girls. As perfect strangers, they shared with us their journey, having sold everything and moved from Switzerland to Redding, California to answer the call of God upon their lives. They had no money, a run down van, and trusted God for every need.

As they shared, God spoke to me and said, "Watch my goodness on display." I looked at their oldest daughter and told the mother, "God is going to open up a modeling and acting opportunity to help with your finances." They were very gracious as they received my words, but even I wasn't so sure where that came from. After our meal, we gladly paid their check and went into the parking lot. As we said good-bye, I heard that familiar voice again, "I'm good Jeremiah, show them." I instantly asked them, "How much food do you have at your house?" They looked down at the ground and said, "None." I said, "Perfect, let's head over to that Target."

We walked into Target with them and took out not one cart… but two! I knew God was being serious about revealing Himself as "good to them" and I wanted to make sure we were honoring His request. We had not walked more than one hundred feet when a woman with long blonde hair stepped out of an aisle and walked right up to the mother. She said, "I'm from a modeling and acting agency and we would like to offer your daughter a job." Stunned, the mother began to cry, as did the young girl. I must say that this is the fastest word of prophecy fulfilled that I have ever given to my knowledge. Could God be such a good Father that He fulfills prophecy within 20 minutes just to show us how good He is? I believe so!

We threw turkey, chicken, milk, you name it into those carts and the more we spent, the more joy I felt inside of my heart. As we made it to their run-down van and put the groceries in the back, we decided to pray them off and get on our way. Yep, you guessed it, the voice again. A free lunch, a modeling job, tons of groceries... but God wasn't done yet showing off His goodness to this dear family in need, that had literally sold everything to obey and follow Him. After prayer, we asked them how much gas they had in the tank.

"EMPTY."

We found ourselves at a gas station nearby filling up their tank and ours. I laughed thinking about "not just a filled tank of gas", but we had received a "full tank of God's goodness" that day. As we finished pumping their gas, a man walked up to us and asked if he could pray for us. We were startled because it seemed he appeared out of nowhere. After how the day had gone, obviously we said, "Yes," and were wondering what would happen next. I'll never forget it, but he went into the circle of the family and the two guys with me and began to prophesy over each one of us. When he got to me, he started shouting and said, "You are about to fall into a night season and write the books God tells you to. And by the way, don't forget about His goodness!"

From one encounter that led to another and another and another and another, God's goodness washed over all of us. That day was an incredible privilege just to partner with God in His desire to show people how good He really is. For Moses, God revealing Himself as good was just not a one time event, God was about to reveal Himself to Moses and His people as good over and over and over again!

Finally, let us not forget that Jesus Christ came to give expression to God's glory, which as we have just read was His goodness. When Jesus Christ walked the earth, He Himself was the full expression of God's goodness upon the earth. There was not guile, wickedness, or deceit found in his mouth (1 Peter 2:22). All who came into contact with Him experienced first hand the goodness of God in its many and varied attributes.

## His Graciousness

The first aspect of God's goodness/glory that He revealed to Moses was His graciousness. Strong's Concordance defines graciousness as: "to bend or stoop in kindness to an inferior, to favor, to deal graciously, to grant graciously, to incline, specifically--to pitch a tent, to encamp for abode, to dwell, to rest in a tent".

When we consider God's desire to dwell with humanity and be near to them, the definition for graciousness here becomes all the more startling. From Jacob's revelation at Bethel to the Tabernacle of Moses to the Tabernacle of David to Solomon's Temple to the restored temple of Zerubbabel, all throughout the Old Testament you have a prophetic picture of God's graciousness being put on display. He pitched a tent with them in the wilderness and eventually provided plans for

Solomon's Temple and others so that He could stoop down toward His people and dwell with them. But He didn't stop there! As we read in John 1:14, John proclaimed and said, *"And the Word became flesh and tabernacled among us, and we beheld His glory..."*

The Son of God, Jesus Christ, became flesh and pitched a tent among humanity that we might receive a revelation of His graciousness toward us as His people! The Father was willing to reach us, through any means, even costing Him the life of His beloved Son so that He might share with us His graciousness. If God Himself is willing to give up what is most precious to Him to reveal His graciousness toward us as sons and daughters, what makes us think that He will reserve and hold back His desires to be gracious toward us as His people? Grace has already been given and paid for! We just have to believe, receive, and release it upon the body of Christ.

Some of my favorite moments of prophetic ministry are when God the Father decides to be incredibly gracious toward individuals. It's as if He sets out to prove to His people that there is no place where He will not go to get on eye to eye level with them, rescue them, and set them free. He got down eye to eye with the woman caught in adultery. He is a God of divine intervention, who takes pleasure in bending and stooping down in kindness to us as inferiors and picking us up, placing us on His lap as Papa and calling us sons and daughters.

## From a Hater to a Lover

When I was in college, I attended a birthday party at a local restaurant in town. As we sat together in the restaurant in a closed off section, I noticed a man who happened to be a server across the room. He was towering around 6'4", had long hair, tattoos and looked visibly upset. I tried to take my eyes off of him, but I just couldn't. God began to share with me part of this man's journey and how broken he was over his family. I knew that he and his sister's relationship was very important to him, and at the time was in disrepair. The birthday party went on and as we sang and ate, I tried to build up courage to talk to this big guy about his sister!

As we were leaving, I saw an opportune moment to introduce myself as I paid my bill. I walked over to him as he was at the cash register and very gently spoke to him what I heard the Father say. Instead of knocking me out, this man began to weep on the job in the middle of the restaurant. He was both shocked and caught off guard. I told him how much Jesus loved Him and that this was God's way of graciously intervening in his situation and bringing healing. I turned around to say goodbye and this guy grabbed me by my arm hard. He said, "Who are you?" I said, "Here's my number and if you want more where that came from, call me."

After his shift that night around midnight, I got a call on my cell phone from this man who was still shaken up. He said, "You don't understand. I'm a God-hater. I've been blaspheming His name for years and making fun of Him. Why is He doing this?" He agreed to meet with me in the morning at a restaurant. The next day he confessed his sins and gave his heart to Jesus Christ. God's graciousness turned a hater into a lover, a blasphemer into a bold preacher of the gospel. Do we really know His grace like we should?

**His Compassion and Mercy**

The second aspect of His Glory and Goodness that God shared with Moses was His compassion/mercy. The Strong's Concordance defines compassion/mercy as:

"from a primitive root 'to fondle,' by implication 'to love; to be compassionate, show mercy, have pity, great tender love, great tender mercy, as a mother cherishes a fetus in the womb.'"

## A Canadian Encounter

There have been many times in my life when I simply felt privileged to witness the mercy and compassion of God moving upon the hearts of men and women. On one particular occasion, I was headed to speak at a prophetic conference in Edmonton, Canada.

I had boarded a half-full flight and was delighted to see that I was the only one seated in my particular row. The plane door shut and I laid my head back to rest. Several minutes later, I was startled as a man, looking exhausted, said he was to be seated right next to me.

I proceeded to strike up a conversation with him and

found out that he was a Canadian pilot who had missed a flight that day and had run through the airport trying to make the flight we were now on. He was assigned another seat, but because they had already shut the door and completed the checklist, he had to be re-issued another ticket as they opened up the plane door again (something he said they never do). His new ticket was the seat right next to me.

Halfway through the flight, I was awakened from my sleep by the voice of the Holy Spirit. He said, "This man's wife is struggling with severe depression and fear. He has also had a very long and hard journey trying to discover who I am. I want you to share with him My mercy and compassion for his life."

I immediately looked over and made eye contact with this man and began by sharing how merciful and compassionate God has been to me in my own life. I shared about his wife and his personal journey as if I had known him all my life.

I cannot really explain what transpired over the course of that flight, up some 30,000 feet in the air, but a man was born into the kingdom of God as the tangible compassion and mercy of God just swept over him. I literally felt so blessed just to be there and watch the Holy Spirit comfort and minister to his broken heart. As He openly confessed Christ as Lord and Savior of His life and repented of His sins, we began to lift up the name of his wife and ask that all depression and fear would leave her life in the name of Jesus.

That Canadian pilot had a real encounter with the mercy and compassion of God that day and so did I myself, being the instrument God had chosen to use. It was the mercy and compassion of God that opened up that plane door a second time and seated this man with over a hundred open seats on a plane right next to me. Let us not lose sight of God opening door after door, divinely placing us next to the right people, just to show us how compassionate and merciful He really is toward our pains and struggles.

Israel was God's firstborn son and He had labored to deliver them from the grips of Egypt. God wanted to grant Moses a revelation of His compassion and mercy so that Moses might walk for the rest of His days with an awareness of how tender and loving He really is. Time and time again in the future of Israel, God would have compassion and mercy upon His people as they strayed and disobeyed Him.

Let us not forget that Jesus Christ came to give expression to the mercy and compassion of God the Father as revealed to Moses in Exodus 34. In all His interactions with humanity, these attributes of God's character and nature touched all    present with Jesus. When four thousand hungry hearts had followed him in Mark 8, Jesus said, "I feel compassion for the multitude because they have remained with Me now for three days, and have nothing to eat; if I send them away hungry to their home, they will faint on the way; and some of them have come from a distance." It is the compassion and mercy of God the Father that if we ask for bread as His sons and daughters, He will not give us stones (Matthew 7:9). God is in the business of lavishing His mercy and compassion upon people and it is extraordinary to be a part of it.

## His Longsuffering

The third aspect of God's glory/goodness that He revealed to Moses was His longsuffering. Strong's Concordance defines longsuffering as: "to be long and drawn out, to lengthen, prolong, to be long-suffering, long-winged, patient, slow to anger (from "flaring the nostrils--from rapid breathing of passion and anger")."

After coming down from Mt. Sinai and discovering that Aaron had made the people a golden calf to worship, Moses was so upset that He smashed the Ten Commandments given to him by Yahweh. After a conversation with God where He wants to blot out the people and start over with Moses, Moses intercedes and asks God to "suffer long" with His people, and that He did. God saw fit to reveal to Moses that an aspect of His character and nature is His ability to be long-suffering with His people, to be patient, to give them time to repent so that Moses could lead the people with an understanding that God Himself is slow to anger.

I remember a season in my life where someone had hurt me very deeply. Some roots of being bitter and unforgiving began to sink into my heart. One night I had a dream where God was about to bless the person who hurt me in a very powerful way. I woke up from the dream upset and said to the Lord, "Please don't ask me to deliver that word Father, I can't."

He responded back and said, "Prophecy has nothing to do with your opinion, son. Yes, he hurt you and yes, I will address that, but I want to share with them my ability to be long-suffering with them." I got up that day and called the person with whom I was upset and asked to meet. As I fought with God about how I felt inside, I took a deep breath and shared the dream that I had with the person. He instantly began to weep because he expected me to release a hard word to him. I was immediately convicted in that moment and decided it was not he that needed to repent, but it was I! After that meeting we became very good friends and to this day still are.

Thank God that He is long suffering with you and I and thank God that He sent His Son Jesus to the earth to be long-suffering with us. As He hung on the cross and said, *"Father, forgive them for they know not what they do,"* surely His long suffering was extended toward us as humanity. When Peter denied Jesus three times and went back to being a fisherman, Jesus did not show up in John 21 and release his wrath upon Peter. Rather he invited him to breakfast and made it an issue of love. Jesus was long-suffering with Peter and is long suffering with you and I!

## His Lovingkindness

The fourth aspect of God's goodness and glory that He shared with Moses was His lovingkindness. Strong's defines "lovingkindness" as: "to be kind, show one's self merciful, beauty, favor, loving-kindness". It's interesting to note that God said, "abounding in lovingkindness". The word "abounding" is a mathematical term meaning "to multiply by the myriads of tens of thousands" and, therefore, to be "abundant, exceedingly enough, plenteous, and sufficient." Such is His lovingkindness and truth.

The Hebrew word for "lovingkindness" here is "chesed," which always carries with it the intention of "loyal, steadfast love". This is God's covenant-keeping love and is used over two hundred and fifty times in the Old Testament. God told Moses that this kind of love was abounding. It was constantly multiplying by the myriads of ten thousands! As God would cry out through his prophets throughout the Old Testament, He would remind them of the covenant that He had made with them, and the covenant-love, the "chesed" out of which it was birthed and sustained.

## Lovingkindness Triumphs

While in Bible college, a friend and I had been meditating on the love of God and its ability to continually pursue us and win our hearts over time and time again even in our rebellion and sin. A specific Scripture that we began to read, pray into, and really put our faith in was Philippians 1:6 which says, *"For I am confident of this very thing, that He who began a good work in you will perfect it until the day of Christ Jesus."*

One night as we were praying together and asking God to give us insight into this particular verse, a frantic knock came to our door. We opened the door and a man said, "A friend just snorted two lines of cocaine in a moment of despair and needs help." My friend and I looked at each other and the loving-kindness of God for this distressed man just overtook us. We asked for directions and sprinted across campus to where he was.

As we entered the door to the room that night and saw this young man who had just snorted a few lines of cocaine thrashing about and writhing in tears and pain, we looked at one another and started shouting Philippians 1:6. We really believed that God was so loving toward this student that what God had started years ago was going to be perfected and even in the drug-induced state, God's love was going to break in.

As we shouted, prayed in tongues, and laid hands upon this brother, an instant miracle took place, like few I've ever seen before. The man went from a totally destructive state with bloodshot red eyes to completely calm and his eyes totally turning clear.

I'll never forget when he said, "What just happened?"

I said, "That was the love of God breaking the power of a drug- induced high off of your life as a sign that you need to repent and get right with Him." As the student wept and told us about his terrible childhood and incredible pain, we cried with him and asked the love of God to continue what He started years ago in this young man's life. We cannot underestimate the depths and lengths that God's love will go to demonstrate that nothing can separate us from His love, not even a drug- induced high!

Jesus Christ became "chesed" for us. He Himself embodied and gave full expression to the lovingkindness of God while He walked the earth. It was for love that He came, in love that He died, and on account of love that He was raised again and now sits at the right hand of the Father interceding and advocating for us.

## His Truth and Trustworthiness

The fifth aspect of His character and nature that He revealed to Moses was His truth/trustworthiness. Strong's Concordance defines "truth/trustworthiness" as: "to build up or support, to foster as a nurse or parent, to trust or believe, permanence, to be true or certain, bring up, establish, of long continuance, therefore, to be trustworthy and faithful."

One of the primary weapons that Satan uses upon the saints of God is deception. It is therefore contained inside of the Father's heart, a deep desire to reveal truth and expose lies. When we believe the lies, we empower the liar, but when we believe what's true, we come to know the God who is full of truth.

I have personally been used in numerous capacities around the world to expose the lies that believers have embraced from the enemy himself to keep them in some form of bondage and unable to fulfill their destiny.

## Lies Exposed

I was ministering to a leadership team at a church in another country who had been through quite a bit of internal attack and assaults from the enemy. One morning as I was ministering to them, I looked at a particular woman and saw the word, "Lie" on her forehead in the spirit. As I inquired of the Lord for an explanation, He told me to tell her that it was not her fault that the church was in the position that it was presently.

I made my way over to the woman and placed my hands upon her head and commanded the lies to leave. I then said, "The black widow is gone, but you are still trapped in her cobwebs." The woman immediately began to sob and the leadership team gasped for air."

The worship leader came over and said, "There was a woman who came to this church some time ago and brought great destruction here and we called her the black widow. The woman you just prayed for invited her here not knowing what would take place and has blamed herself ever since."

The God of truth came and broke off a satanic lie in that woman's mind that day and set her free to forgive herself and walk forward in her destiny. God is constantly and consistently wanting to expose us to the truth of His Word and the truth of who He really is.

It was important to God to share with Moses that He was full of truth and trustworthy in every way. It was not God Himself who needed to know this, but Moses. God is faithful and true to His word and promises and many times He chooses to remind us of this in our journey to know Him. It is because He is truthful that He is trustworthy. He said elsewhere, "God is not a man, that He should lie, nor a son of man that He should repent; has He said and will He not do it? Or has He spoken and will He not make it good?"

Jesus Christ came to the earth not only full of grace, but also full of truth (John 1:14). These two aspects of His character and nature cannot be divorced from one another. He is trustworthy in every way and ultimately demonstrated this by doing everything that He told the disciples He would do, even to the point of dying on a cross.

**His Forgiveness**

The sixth aspect of God's character and nature that He shared with Moses was His forgiveness. He said, *"The LORD...who forgives iniquity, transgression, and sin"* (Exodus 34:7).

God wanted Moses to know that part of His nature is that He is the forgiver of sins! We know in the Old Testament that God pardoned sins based upon the Law, and the shedding of the blood of bulls and goats. However, they were never really "taken away, swept away and removed" until the Lamb of God appeared, of whom John declared, *"Behold, the Lamb of God who 'takes away' the sin of the world"* (John 1:29). Under the New Covenant in His blood, it was ultimately His will that He might *"remember our sins no more"* (Jeremiah 31:31; Hebrews 8:12; 10:17), through the "one time" and "once for all" sacrifice of the Lamb (Hebrews 9:27-29).

## His Justness

The seventh and final attribute of His goodness and Glory, and therefore His character and nature shown and declared to Moses was His justness. As mentioned earlier, this is based upon His rightness and correctness, and the final statement of the LORD Himself: *"...yet He shall by no means leave the guilty unpunished, visiting the iniquity of the fathers on the children and the grandchildren to the third and fourth generations."* God's justness is part of His goodness, part of His Glory, part of His character, and part of His nature. He said in another place, *"For I, the LORD, do not change"* (Malachi 3:6).

Contrary to the current opinions of many well-known and reputable men, some of whom are prophets themselves, the New Covenant does not change the character and nature of the One who cannot change. Neither does this Covenant cancel out or take out of play the justness of God! It remains an eternal Attribute of His Goodness. His justness is not contrary to His goodness: it is part of His goodness! To deny that reality is to misrepresent the character and nature of His goodness and glory. (In that we shall speak more on this later in the book, we will leave it at that for now).

## Our Access Point

In case you're still wondering, the character and nature of God has everything to do with prophetic ministry. In fact, the ultimate purpose of God releasing His gifts, the prophets to His corporate body, is to assist them in their journey to be conformed to His image and likeness! When people leave prophetic conferences and gatherings, they should sense and feel that what they have received will primarily assist them in the inward character transformation that God the Father so desires for their lives. If we do not truly know Him, what He is really like, how can we represent Him to the people with integrity? As prophetic people, if we pick and choose certain aspects of His character and nature that we want to share with His people and choose to ignore or disregard others, our quivers will not be full of who He truly is and the arrows that we release will greatly limit His impact upon the saints.

## Releasing His Character and Nature

The character and nature of God must be our access point into all that the Father will and would want to speak to His children. When I am asked to prophesy over individuals, I do not connect with their spirit through soulish means. Rather, I connect to the character and nature of God and release to them through the Father's heart and not mine what He wants to say to them. Much of what I am currently seeing in the prophetic movement is nothing more than psychic reading and fortune telling. We have watered down prophetic ministry in America to reading people's hearts back to them. When we do not truly know the God of the Scriptures, we will seek to connect our human spirit to another's spirit and base the prophetic words we give off of our own experience. This is not only dangerous, but involves the spirit of witchcraft because it's born out of the flesh and will always involve various forms of manipulation and control because it's self-serving.

I see a new breed of prophets leading a new prophetic generation who will stand in the council of the Lord and when asked to prophesy, they will read the Father's heart back to people because they have chosen to make their home there. These individuals with not only be a tremendous refreshing to the body of Christ, but extremely rare in the days ahead. They will not confirm the selfish-ambitions of people nor will they aid individuals in their fleshly pursuits of success as defined by the world. This new prophetic generation will be like Micaiah in 1 Kings 22:14 who said to King Ahab, *"As the Lord lives, what the Lord says to me, that I will speak."*

When God does not speak, they will not speak. When He speaks they will deliver every word regardless of how well it is received or their personal experience with God. This new prophetic generation will learn how to embrace every aspect of His character and nature and will not be dissuaded or manipulated by the opinions of men. They will find themselves connected to pastors and leaders in strategic locations in the United States who genuinely want to receive the Father's Heart and words, regardless of the necessary changes and corrections that must to take place because of the words spoken. Just as Jesus declared in Matthew 4:4, there will be regions of the United States that *"will not live on bread alone, but on every word that comes from the mouth of God. "*

They will invite with open arms this new prophetic generation who will only speak His words and count them a blessing rather than a curse. Intercessors will weep and wail as the true words of the Father fall like fire upon the altar of dry and weary hearts. The greatest days of the prophetic movement are right around the corner. They will be full of an exposing of that which is counterfeit, carnal, and self-serving and a release of a new prophetic generation who have been hidden, consecrated, and forged in the fire for such a time as this.

## Down From the Mountain

As Moses came down from Mt. Sinai after encountering the answer to His inquiry, *"Show me your glory, "* His face was full of radiant light. Exodus 34:30 says, *"So when Aaron and all the sons of Israel saw*

*Moses, behold, the skin of his face shone, and they were afraid to come near him.*" When the people got over their fears and allowed Moses to speak to them, the passage goes on to say, *"When Moses had finished speaking with them, he put a veil over his face. But whenever Moses went in before the Lord to speak with Him, he would take off the veil until he came out; and whenever he came out and spoke to the sons of Israel, they would see that His face was shining and he would put a veil on to cover his face."*

The character and nature of God had so made its mark upon Moses that no man could look upon his face without being afraid. Therefore he saw it fit to cover his face as he spoke with the people. What really happened up on that mountain? Let us not forget that the hand of God had put him in the cleft of a rock and even covered him as He passed by because as God has said, *"You cannot see My face,* for no man can see Me and live!" (Exodus 33:20).

While it was impossible to encounter the fullness of God's glory in His Face and still live, and even though Moses could only see the backside of the LORD as He passed before him proclaiming the qualities of His character and nature, Yahweh still made *"all My goodness"* pass through Moses as well. No man had ever seen or experienced what Moses did that day on that mountain. Moses got lit up! So much so that his face shone with the radiant splendor of God's glory. Is it not a total mystery and wonder then that John declared of the incarnate Word in John 1:14, *"we beheld His glory,"* and in Hebrews 1:3 it says that *"Jesus is the radiance of the Father's glory!"*

What Moses saw and experienced only briefly and somewhat partially was now fully seen and recognized in the "True Light" Himself, Jesus Christ in the New Testament. Furthermore, while Moses' face was transformed by the glory of God that faded away with time, our inward parts *"are continually being transformed into the same image, from glory to glory, just as from the Lord, the Spirit"* (2 Corinthians 3:18). As Paul wrote in 2 Corinthians 3:11, *"For if that which fades away was with glory, how much more that which remains is in glory?"*

## The Testimony of Jesus

The goodness of God, His graciousness, His unending compassion and mercy, His longsuffering with humanity, His abounding lovingkindness, His truth and trustworthiness, His marvelous heart to forgive and remember no more, and justness were all completely portrayed by the God-Man Jesus Christ as He walked the earth two thousand years ago. Goodness held hands and laughed with the disciples by the Sea of Galilee. By its very definition it (goodness) means beautiful, delightful, glad and joyous. This is He of whom King David wrote in Song of Solomon 5:10 when he said, *"He is the fairest of ten thousand."* Graciousness bent down to write in the sand while He got on eye-to-eye level with a woman caught in adultery. The compassionate and merciful One saw the crowds of people and would not send them away hungry. His ability to be longsuffering met Peter and the disciples when He made them breakfast on the beach, rather than go on a tirade for why they had betrayed and deserted Him (John21).

Lovingkindness, covenant love, went to the cross for you and I. He became "chesed" for us in every sense of the word. Truth stood before Pontius Pilate before His death and declared, *"Everyone who is of the truth hears My voice"* (John 18:37). Forgiveness was crucified to a tree. When they spat upon Him and ridiculed Him, He said, *"Father, forgive them for they know not what they do."* Justness reminded the Pharisees in Matthew 12:33-37 that they would have to give an account on the day of judgment for every careless word they had spoken.

It is this testimony of Jesus, as revealed in the Scriptures, that is the spirit of prophecy (Revelation 19:10). The true "testimony of Jesus" is that which reveals His true Person, His real character and nature. Not just the part of Him (in John 8) that told the woman caught in adultery that He did not condemn her, but also the part of Him that told her, *"go and sin no more."* Not just the Jesus that is full of grace, but also the Jesus that is full of truth (John 1:14). Not just a Jesus who was full of goodness in that He was morally and motivationally pure, and had no guile, wickedness, or deceit found in His mouth (1 Peter 2:22). But also a Jesus who was so good (right and correct) that He had no issue with bringing correction to the Pharisees and religious leaders on countless occasions in the Scriptures (Matthew 23).

The new prophetic generation rising up in the earth will carry 2 Corinthians 3:18 like a banner as it says, *"But we all, with unveiled face beholding as in a mirror the glory of the Lord, are being transformed into the same image from glory to glory, just as from the Lord, the Spirit."* This new prophetic generation will not settle with being touched by God, but have committed to being changed deeply and inwardly by His Spirit. They have not settled for a gospel of behavior modification and sin management, nor will they prophesy of one. They not only hunger for the power of God that releases the miracles of God, but they seek His dealings that produce His character. Because of this, there is not a part of God's character and nature that they run from in their personal lives, nor are they afraid to share those dealings of His character formation within themselves with the body of Christ in the public place.

I'm convinced with all my heart that what the body of Christ needs most from the new prophetic generation are messengers that will simply introduce Jesus Christ, rather than try to produce Him to the people. God does not need makeup nor does He need anyone trying to tie his shoes or straighten His tie. The role of a prophetic person is so far from trying to do a PR job for God, and what we are witnessing in much of the prophetic movement is just that. In brokenness, error, and limited experiences, we are attempting to divorce the God of the Old Testament from the God of the New Testament. The source of confusion lies at the foot of the cross. Did the death, burial, and resurrection of Jesus Christ change the purpose and content of prophecy forever? Are there aspects of God's character and nature in the Old Testament that are no longer active and necessary in the New Testament? The answers to these difficult questions are answered in the following pages. Keep reading!

# - 3 -
# NEW COVENANT PROPHECY

The greatest area of conflict in the prophetic movement is over the issue of New Covenant prophecy versus Old Covenant prophecy. In keeping with the content of this book, the argument is tied right back into our revelation and interpretation of the character and nature of God.

## Prophetic Collision

I remember it like it was yesterday. I was 19 and hungry to rub shoulders with some "well known prophets" in the earth. I had read online about a conference in Mechanicsburg, Pennsylvania called the "Voice of the Prophets" and immediately knew I needed to be in attendance. Having hardly any finances as a Bible college student, I decided to buy a round trip airfare ticket with the only money I had. I would need to believe God to somehow get me to the conference from the airport, find me a place to stay, provide some food to eat, and registration for the meetings. Little did know that that I was in for an experience of a lifetime!

As I sat in the Mechanicsburg airport with a large poster that read, "Looking for a ride to the prophets conference", hours and hours went by. Some people stopped and asked where I was headed, but no one was passing through the area where the conference was being held. Suddenly and to my great surprise, a man named Dave walked right up to me with a huge smile and said, "I'm headed to the prophets conference, come with me."

Complete strangers, I jumped in a rental car with my new friend Dave and he proceeded to pay for my hotel, food, and even conference registration for the next 4 days. It was truly a miracle and I have never forgotten the experience, but something even greater took place that has influenced me more to this day than perhaps most other encounters I've had.

On the second night of the conference, two of the prophets who had been speaking at several sessions ended up having a very heated discussion in the back of the auditorium. I had the opportunity and privilege to witness the debate and have been profoundly impacted ever since. One prophet said to other, "I disagree with your message brother; it was full of judgment. We are in a prophetic season of grace. God judged Jesus on the cross and will judge us when the books are opened in eternity, but between then and now, we live in a season of grace. There is no room for judgment now." The prophet looked at the prophet who had just spoken and said, "Have you read the book of Revelation chapters 2 and 3 where a resurrected Jesus is rebuking five out of seven churches for their immorality and complacency? All you prophets say there is no more judgment since Jesus Christ died on the Cross and you could not be more wrong!"

These two men carried on and on and then left without shaking hands or in one bit of agreement. Having witnessed the whole ordeal at 19, I was deeply shaken to the core. At that point in time, I had no idea how opinionated and divided the prophetic movement really is over the issue of judgment in the New Covenant. Years removed from this event and the more I minister prophetically and interact with prophets from across the world, this conversation mentioned seems to be THE issue!

If the foundation for all prophetic ministry is built

upon the character and nature of God, then we have to know Him to rightly represent Him to the people. Many prophets and prophetic people have no problem acknowledging a God in the Old Testament that was full of wrath and judgment, but numerous ones have an issue regarding a God in the New Testament who disciplines, judges and corrects, much less a God who is still full of wrath and judgment.

What does this have to do with prophesying over individuals, nations, and ministries? EVERYTHING! When prophets are prophesying, they are doing more than releasing God's words. They are releasing His character and nature into the atmosphere and into people's lives. They are declaring, "THIS IS WHAT GOD IS REALLY LIKE!"

## Old Testament Versus New Testament

As we discovered in the second chapter, Jesus Christ in the New Testament, came to be the full expression of every aspect of the character and nature of the God of the Old Testament, as revealed to Moses in Exodus 34. God was not just a Good God in the Old Testament and then said, "I will not be that way in the New Testament." Nor did He say, "I am full of truth," in the New Testament and then show Himself to not be like that in the Old Testament. I want to be very clear and transparent: the current pursuit by prophets in the earth right now to divorce the God of the Old Testament away from the God of the New Testament is perhaps doing more damage to the body of Christ than any other endeavor.

We are not only creating confusion in the minds and hearts of the body of Christ, but we are creating division within the prophetic movement. Is it not strange that some prophets are declaring that judgment is right around the corner for America and others at the very same time are saying that America is headed for the biggest revival and awakening we have ever known? Which ones are right and which ones are wrong, or are they both right or are they both wrong?

Our answers to these difficult questions are going to be directly affected by our revelation and interpretation of the character and nature of God as revealed in the Scriptures. The new prophetic generation rising in the earth is going to give themselves to a wholehearted and radical pursuit of discovering who God is like no generation of prophetic people before them. Rather than divorcing the God of the Old Testament from the God of the New Testament, this new prophetic generation will give their lives to see them united as one! As Hebrews

13:8 says, *"Jesus Christ is the same yesterday, today, and forever."* Handling the Word of God with integrity and refusing to search the Scriptures to confirm their own experiences, but rather using the Scriptures to discern any errors in their experiences will mark this new prophetic generation.

## Rejecting or Responding

As God revealed seven aspects of His character and nature to Moses in Exodus 34:7, He finished revealing Himself by saying, *"who keeps lovingkindness for thousands, who forgives iniquity, transgressions, and sins, yet He will by no means leave the guilty unpunished, visiting the iniquity of the fathers on the children and on the grandchildren to the third and fourth generation."*

In order to fully understand how God is revealing Himself to Moses in Exodus 34, it is important to note that there are two groups of people that God is directing Himself towards in this portion of Scripture. There are those who respond to His truth and there are those who reject it. It is to those who reject the truth of God in the Old Testament that He will "by all means not leave unpunished."

Exodus 34:7 is an expansion of the chesed/love and emet/truth balance that is at the core of God's character and nature. In fact, sixteen times in the Old Testament, love and truth are wrapped together in a bundle. If the people responded to God in repentance and love---He would keep hesed for thousands of generations and forgive their iniquity, transgressions and sins. God's lovingkindness in the Old Testament was reserved for those who responded rightly to His truth. But to those that refused His truth, they also forsook His love and they by all means were not left unpunished.

In Exodus 20:5 it says, *"You shall not worship them or serve them; for I, the Lord your God, am a jealous God, visiting the iniquity of the fathers on the children, on the third and the fourth generation of those who hate Me, but showing lovingkindness to those who love Me and keep my commandments."* God's dealings with His people under the Old Covenant were entirely dependent upon their response to the truth of His word. To those that hated God, He would visit the iniquity of the fathers on the children to the third and fourth generation. To those who loved Him and kept His commands, He would show His lovingkindness towards them.

Proverbs 1:23-31 is a powerful parallel passage that continues to drive home this understanding of the character and nature of God as it says,

*"Turn to my reproof. Behold, I will pour out My Spirit on you; I will make my words known to you. Because I called, and you refused, I stretched out my hand and no one paid attention and you neglected my counsel, and did not want my reproof; I will even laugh at your calamity; I will mock when your dread comes, When your dread comes like a storm, and your calamity comes like a whirlwind, when distress and anguish come on you. Then they will call on me, but I will not answer; they will seek me diligently, but they shall not find me, because they hated knowledge, and did not choose to fear the Lord. They would not accept my counsel and they spurned all my reproof. So they shall eat the fruit of their own way."*

This passage of Scripture is directly focused on the response of the people to God's interactions and dealings with them. It is clear according to the Old Testament, that God's judgment was reserved for those who rejected His truth and therefore forsook His love. He would not leave those guilty ones unpunished and the entirety of the Old Testament is proof of just that reality.

If this is how God dealt with humanity under the Old Covenant, according to how they responded to His truth and words, how then does He deal with His people under the New Covenant? Is there any type of judgment reserved for not only unbelievers who hate him, but also believers in Christ who forsake His commandments and stray from the path?

Let's take a look at 1 Corinthians 11, as Paul

addresses the saints in regards to partaking of the Lord's Supper. In 11:29-32 he says, *"For he who eats and drinks, eats and drinks judgment to himself, if he does not judge the body rightly. For this reason many among you are weak and sick, and a number sleep. But if we judged ourselves rightly, we should not be judged. But when we are judged, we are disciplined by the Lord in order that we may not be condemned along with the world."*

Paul is sharing with the believers at Corinth that if they do not partake of the Lord's supper out of having judged their own hearts and motives rightly, then God Himself would judge them and that His judgment is His discipline for their lives.

God is portrayed under the New Covenant as one who disciplines His children, as any good father will do diligently. On multiple occasions in the New Testament, the Father Himself is the disciplinarian in His family of sons. In fact, in Hebrews 12:5-11, He instructs believers to not take His discipline lightly, and not to faint when reproved by Him, because *"those whom He loves He disciplines and He scourges every son whom He receives."* In this passage the writer equates the discipline of the Father as both the proof of His fatherhood and the proof of our being His sons! Mature sons acknowledge both of these realities, while sons who still live out of an orphan-heart view any idea of being disciplined as somehow being rejected by God. In both 1 Corinthians 11 and Hebrews 12, discipline is considered a type of judgment that God releases upon the lives of believers when they do not respond to Him in a way that pleases Him.

## A Change of Position

I believe God is positioning the bride of Christ in this hour to a place where they will receive His correction, discipline, rebuke and therefore His justness without interpreting it as rejection. His judgment upon our lives is a demonstration of His goodness toward us as His people. The issue is not over whether He loves us, but over whether our own orphan heart's can receive His love for us. At times the words of the Father bring great comfort to our hearts and in other seasons His words sting in order to bring adjustment. We must always remember that whether the words comfort or sting, they are still coming from the same voice of our loving Father!

When the post-resurrected Jesus spoke to the believers at Laodicea, He said to them in Revelation

3:19, *"Those whom I love I rebuke and discipline. So be earnest and repent."* The same Greek word for "judgment" in 1 Corinthians 11 is the same word here for discipline. In other words Jesus said, "Those whom I love I rebuke and judge."

## An Encounter With Jesus Christ

On April 6, 2013, I had one of the most terrifying dreams of my life as the Lord Jesus Christ was standing in front of me in my bedroom wearing a white robe and having fire in His eyes. In the dream, a man was standing next to me and Jesus pointed to him and said, "I have created you for the ministry. Why are you not doing what I asked you to do?"

As this question was asked, this man began to tremble, and so did I. Jesus extended His arms towards us and a wave of scorching fire consumed us. That is the only way I know how to describe what happened. As the fire hit me, and this man in the dream, I immediately woke up in my bed soaked in sweat, and I looked over at the clock and it was 3:33 am.

Catching my breath and listening to the silence in the room, I heard the voice of the Father as He said to me, "I am going to baptize this generation with the fire of My discipline and chastisement because I love them and because they refuse to do what I have asked them to do." I began to weep as the Father told me this and I said to Him, "What has this generation done to warrant chastisement and discipline because this is not the primary way that you deal with us as your children?"

The Holy Spirit immediately reminded me as I sat in the bed that night of 1Corinthians 11:29-32 and highlighted verses 31 and 32 as they say, *"But if we judged ourselves rightly, we should not be judged. But when we are judged, we are disciplined by the Lord in order that we may not be condemned along with the world."*

The God of the Old Testament punished His people because there was no sacrifice for sins that could satisfy His wrath. The God of the New Testament disciplines His people because there was a complete sacrifice for their sins that could satisfy His wrath. His name is Jesus Christ.

"The discipline of the Lord," whether the discipline of the Lord Jesus or the discipline of the LORD God Almighty (the Father) upon the life of the believer must not be seen as punishment, but rather that which separates the precious from the vile. The discipline of the Father upon His children is an act of love for their own good! God does rebuke, He does correct, and He does bring adjustment to our lives as believers under the New

Covenant as part of His character and nature that we might share in His holiness (Hebrews 12:10).

I want to be clear, while I do not believe that correction and discipline (judgment) is the primary way God deals with us as His children under the New Covenant, to throw out these aspects of His character and nature all together and say that the cross of Jesus Christ did away with them is heretical and not founded upon the full council of God. As prophetic people, we must take careful consideration and observation of ALL SCRIPTURE before we make blanket statements. God is a good and gracious Father, but He will in His truth and justness bring about correction and discipline for our good. As Hebrews 12:6 says, *"For those whom the Lord loves He disciplines and He scourges every son whom He receives."*

## Distorted and Twisted Views

One of the greatest obstacles and hindrances to prophets and prophetic people accepting a New Covenant God that can and will discipline believers is a completely distorted view of the cross of Jesus Christ. To say that under the New Covenant that there is no more room for judgment and particularly no more room for the discipline of God upon the life of a believer is not only biblically inaccurate, but it also brings forth a potential greater underlying issue, namely that we can become so enamored and obsessed with certain aspects of God's character and nature, that we totally disregard those that have the potential to be offensive to people.

In some prophetic circles, there is such an emphasis and focus being placed on the goodness and kindness of God, that anything in any prophetic word that even remotely speaks of God the Father's ability to bring correction and rebuke as His discipline to His people's lives is almost categorically rejected. Warnings, cautions, and anything whatsoever considered negative is thrown out the window as not being part of New Covenant prophecy.

Prophetic words that address specific sin, call for repentance on a personal, city, or national level are frowned upon because they are considered judgmental. Many believe God is not into that anymore. As prophets and prophetic people, if we believe that God as Father is incapable of disciplining His kids, every prophetic word we release, regardless of how a person is responding to the truth of God in their lives, will assure them that only blessing and hope are around the corner. No where in scripture does God promise peace, prosperity, and blessing to individuals, ministries, and nations who walk according to the council of the wicked.

In other prophetic circles, there is such an emphasis being placed on the judgment and correction of God, that any word that remotely speaks of God's desire as Father to bring healing and restoration to His people is categorically rejected. Prophetic words filled with destiny, hope, and the promise of an awakening, are thrown out the window because God is now fed up with the sin of the people. As prophetic voices, if we believe that God the Father is incapable of demonstrating His kindness and goodness to His people, every prophetic word that we release, regardless of how a person is responding to the truth of God in their lives, will carry an unnecessary corrective and judgmental tone to it.

The new prophetic generation rising in the earth will not only know God the Father as a good and kind God, but also a God and Father who disciplines because He loves. Whether it's a word of rebuke and correction or a word of affirmation and applause, they will not reject certain aspects of God's character and nature and accept others. They will not be limited by their personal experience and will take into consideration the full council of God as they sit before Him.

We all have to ask ourselves as prophets and prophetic people, "What arrows do I have in my quiver and what arrows do I need to receive?" What aspects of God's character and nature do I currently understand, and therefore am capable of releasing to His people and what aspects of His character and nature quite frankly make me uncomfortable, and therefore limit me in my ability to minister to His people? Have I had hurtful experiences in the past that prevent me from receiving all of who God is?

No doubt, the new prophetic generation led by a new

breed of prophets will carry quivers that are full of an unusual amount of arrows. They are not only capable of prophesying incredible words of hope, destiny, and healing, but they are also trained in releasing words of correction, rebuke, and calls for repentance.

While prophets and people alike simply cannot fully comprehend this God of the Old Testament and God of the New Testament, this new prophetic generation will carry a rare grace to see them as one. They will testify that Jesus is not only full of grace, but also full of truth. They will testify that God the Father not only loves His children, but loves them enough to discipline them when they go astray. This new prophetic generation will know what the people of God need and when they need it. Just as an earthly father knows what his children need and when they need it, so this new prophetic generation will be keenly aware of the Father's heart and have access to

His mind and His emotions. I see indescribable beauty and testimonies too numerous to count as these messengers travel the earth rebuking and correcting one and releasing the Father's goodness and kindness to another. You won't have to worry, because to them, they are still representing the same loving Father regardless of how He chooses to manifest Himself. And oh my, how full their quivers shall be!

## Maturing in the Prophetic

I want to try and articulate the very best way that I can that to continue majoring on certain aspects of God's character and nature and to minor or plainly ignore others is both unhealthy and it leaves the prophetic movement greatly limited and ineffective in its impact on the body of Christ. Some prophetic people have an exceedingly great revelation of the kindness and graciousness of God, while others possess an immeasurable grace to deliver words full of correction and rebuke.

We must not lift up and magnify certain aspects of who God is to the degree that the people of God become totally unfamiliar and uncomfortable with other aspects. Whether God's goodness and kindness make them uneasy or His ability to correct and bring adjustment makes them cringe, we must give ourselves to allowing God the Father to work into us the aspects of His character and nature that we do not yet possess. A fully mature prophetic person will carry and embrace every aspect of the character and nature of God and be graced with the ability to deliver at any moment to any individual the portion of who God is that the person is in need of.

We must see the prophetic ministry as God inviting His people through His servants into a full-on participation and encounter with His character and nature, rather than being spectators of the words He releases. I see prophetic schools in the days ahead spending way more time teaching prophetic people about the character and nature of God, and way less time on the mechanics of prophecy. Our desires in the prophetic movement to get words of knowledge for people and various details of their lives to produce a "wow factor" has totally derailed God's desires to impart His character and nature to His people.

Once again, one of the primary roles of a prophetic voice is to assist people in their ultimate calling in life, which is to be conformed into the image of Jesus Christ, the Son. (Romans 8:29) In essence, we have too many prophetic voices ready to tell people **what** God wants to do for them and not enough messengers ready to tell people **who** God wants to be for them. I remind you as the reader, that Moses as the leader of Israel in Exodus 33 and 34 could not have been more ripe for a word of direction and future promises. Most prophetic voices would have jumped at an opportunity to prophesy to a man leading a one million man army, knowing what God had already spoken! But what does God Himself choose to release to Moses? His character and nature! It wasn't **what** God could do for Moses that would get him to his destiny, but **who** God could be for Moses that would grant him access to His destiny for him. And let's not forget, God shared **all** of who He was to Moses. He did not hide or ignore certain aspects of His character and nature to Moses, but rather He showed all of Himself to him and even more so to us as believers in the Person of Jesus Christ as revealed in the New Testament.

## Prophets and the Gift of Prophecy

I believe one of the most misunderstood aspects of God's character and nature under the New Covenant is His ability to bring discipline to His people and how it relates to the prophetic ministry. In 1 Corinthians 14:3 Paul gives clear instruction regarding the gift of prophecy as he says, *"But the one who prophesies speaks to men for edification, exhortation, and consolation."*

It's important to understand that there is a **difference** between those who operate in the gift of prophecy on occasion and those who have been called to the ministry of a New Testament prophet. Paul is clearly placing limits and restrictions in 1 Corinthians 14 on those who have the gift of prophecy by telling them that the only types of words that they can release in public meetings must be full of "edification, exhortation, and consolation." I believe that words of correction and rebuke are reserved only for those who have been called by God to the ministry of a New Testament prophet. Why? Because God can only entrust His words of discipline and correction to His servants the prophets, who understand true brokenness and humility. The very idea that any individual can deliver the discipline of the Lord to an individual, ministry, or nation with a smile on their face and a self-righteous heart is a clear indicator that they are not a trusted or tested vessel of the Father Himself. They are immature, arrogant, and do not know the Heart of the Father.

Jeremiah the prophet is an excellent example of a man called under the Old Covenant to deliver very hard words from God to the people, but yet He was known as a weeping prophet. Jeremiah was not only a prophet that mourned over the sin of the people, but even more so, he was a man that got caught up in the heart of a weeping Father who desired the affection and obedience of His children.

## Delivering Corrective Words of Prophecy

While I believe that words of discipline from the Father are only reserved for New Testament prophets and not for those who operate in an occasional gift of prophecy, I also believe that corrective words of prophecy should never be delivered spontaneously in a public gathering. I have rarely seen a corrective word of prophecy that was delivered in this manner bear fruit, not only because it was released in the wrong setting, but it was so vague that it created more confusion than clarity.

As a believer who operates in the gift of prophecy, if all you are ever delivering and receiving are words of correction and rebuke for people, you need to go back and read 1 Corinthians 14 and while you're at it, cry out for a revelation of the character and nature of God. And if you are called to be a New Testament prophet and all you ever release are hard and judgmental words toward leaders and the body of Christ, your quiver is not full and you need to embrace every aspect of God's character and nature, so that those who sit under your ministry might receive a mature and complete revelation of who God is!

The fact that church leadership has to worry about some bizarre prophet walking into the back of the church building (and of course no one has ever seen them before) and rebuking the leadership for hidden sin or a number of different issues is completely out of alignment with the heart of the Father for the New Testament church. A prophet's behavior should put a ministry team at ease, rather than on the edge of their seats with unnecessary fear. New Covenant prophets have been sent to local assemblies to be blessings rather than collateral damage!

With all of this being said, I absolutely believe that there is a place for corrective prophecy regarding the discipline of the Lord under the New Covenant, but it must never be given spontaneously and only delivered by broken and tested prophets. The issue at stake here is how to effectively steward corrective words from the Father in a way that will bring forth the greatest amount of fruit. Standing up in the back of a church building unannounced and starting to shout or grabbing a microphone and screaming will not have a far- reaching impact upon the saints. Ultimately, it will be destructive rather than becoming a blessing to an assembly of believers, which again is not the heart of the Father for the New Testament Church.

Protocol and strategy must be established in a local

assembly by church leadership to provide a place for tested and broken prophets to submit corrective words of prophecy. I believe that how we deliver a word must be seen as a key ingredient in the fulfillment of it. I see a new breed of prophets coming forth in the earth that are seasoned and broken vessels that the Father can entrust with strong corrective words for individuals, ministries, and nations, because it is an aspect of His character and nature that He chooses to share with His people. This, as Hebrews 12:10 says, *"...is for our good that we may share in His holiness"*.

I would like to encourage prophetic people and also those who have been called to the ministry of a New Testament prophet that oftentimes God will reveal the shortcomings of others to you, not for ammunition against them, but as information on how to pray for them. If we would take the sin that we see in other people, ministries, and nations and allow God the Father to work His character and nature inside of us, we could never again deliver a corrective word from a place of arrogance, self-righteousness, or pride.

As prophets, we must constantly be on guard that our "corrective words from God" are not actually born from the spirits of accusation and suspicion. The enemy operates in vagueness. He constantly whispers that there is sin in the camp, but never gives any specifics. I believe with all my heart that an aspect of God's character and nature as revealed in the New Testament is His ability to train, adjust, correct, and rebuke, but we must be very careful as prophets that we are spending significant time with Him in prayer and fasting to allow Him to work His Heart inside of us before we deliver His words. It is not enough to deliver His words, we must deliver them with His heart!

The abuse and misuse of this particular aspect of God's character and nature has done a tremendous amount of damage to the body of Christ and the prophetic movement itself. On the other hand, we are also witnessing an over-emphasis being placed on God's goodness and kindness to the total disregard for His ability to discipline and bring correction to His body. And this, in part, because so many prophets that have gone before us have prophesied out of their flesh and not from spending time standing in the council of the Lord and allowing His Character and Nature to be fully formed inside of them.

I believe in order for the prophetic movement to put childish ways behind them and truly grow up in this hour, we are going to have to stop letting the extremes of our past experiences dictate our present and future beliefs of who God is and how we are to minister His character and nature to His people. Just because the prophets of the past may have prophesied about a God who was angry when really He was delighted, does not mean we should currently prophesy about a God who is pleased when really He is upset or vice versa. As prophets, we must set aside the extremes and even our own experiences and go on a journey to discover His character and nature as revealed in His scripture. It is only through spending time with Him that we will carry an accurate revelation and interpretation of who He is and release it to the saints.

# - 4 -

# CHARACTER TRANSFORMATION

The new prophetic generation being revealed in the earth will not only wholeheartedly give themselves to the knowledge of who God is, but they will walk with character that matches anointing. In fact, the new prophetic generation believes that character trumps anointing.

I was in the Garden of Gethsemane while visiting Israel in May of 2014 and as I was deep in prayer and meditation, the Holy Spirit spoke to me and said, "If you do not deal with your flesh privately, your flesh will deal with you publicly. This is what has happened to many prophets that have gone before you."

I believe God the Father is raising up a new prophetic

generation that is going to seek to put to death every idea in people's minds regarding words that are associated with prophets and the prophetic movement. I see strategic days in the body of Christ that are quickly approaching where synonyms for a new prophetic generation that carries the glory and anointing of God will be: holy, uncompromised, righteous, loving their spouse as Christ loved the church, above reproach, not lovers of money, and most of all; radically given over to character transformation.

One of the most grievous sins of the prophetic movement in the past has been the acceptance of powerful gifting and huge moral flaws as a packaged deal. We have been deceived into believing that we cannot walk in the anointing of the Holy Spirit and the power of God without having huge character issues that must be addressed. This type of thinking does not reflect the ministry of Jesus Christ in any way. How many more Christian leaders are going to use the example of David and Bathsheba as to why their affair is okay? Do we realize that the Bible is full of flawed individuals to show us how much we really need Jesus, the model of perfection, instead of using the sin of a Bible character to excuse our sin? The new prophetic generation is going to fix its eyes upon Jesus and His sinless life and example like no other generation before them. They will define success in the prophetic ministry not based on how accurately they can prophesy or how many dreams and visions they've had, but on how well they are submitting to being conformed to the image and likeness of Jesus Christ.

The new prophetic generation will be taught by a new breed of prophets who will accurately instruct them in the revelation that God is more interested in **changing them** than **using them**. Some of the most prophetically gifted individuals that I personally know are also some of the most emotionally unstable people that I know. These men and women have been wounded by numerous leaders and family members and are convinced that God is more interested in opening up ministry doors for them than leading them to the foot of the Cross to find inner healing and deliverance.

## Holy Father

There is a direct connection between our revelation of who God is and its immediate application in our lives. In other words, people operate their lives according to their revelation of who God is. Much of the immorality and sin that we are currently witnessing and have witnessed in the prophetic movement is directly connected to a misunderstanding and often times distorted perception of who God is. Many are currently voicing a revelation of God being "Father" that somehow now excuses their sin, rather than confronting it in love. Connecting the revelation of "Yahweh" in the Old Testament and "Father" in the New Testament has proven to be a very difficult task for this current prophetic culture.

In the midst of the confusion of who God is in the 21st Century and its direct effect upon the lives of people, Jesus Christ Himself gave us revelation and insight into who God really is in John 17:11 as he said, *"...Holy Father, keep them in your name which you have given me, that they may be one, even as We are."* We must understand as the new prophetic generation that God is not just "Holy," nor is He just "Father." He indeed must be embraced, received, and related to as "Holy Father."

As our Holy Father, He invites us into a love

relationship where He tenderly and affectionately affirms and speaks destiny over our lives. But make no mistake about this: He is also the same God who will remove everything in our lives that hinders His love because He is Holy. I warn you, beware of false prophets in the earth who are divorcing the "Holy Father". He is not one or the other, He is both/ and.

## Hallowed Be Thy Name

I believe the very reason why the greatest need in the prophetic movement right now is to embrace every aspect of God's Character and Nature is because it is directly affecting the moral decisions that prophetic people and the body of Christ are making. Paul appealed to the believers at Ephesus in Ephesians 5:1 and said, "Therefore be imitators (mimics) of God, as beloved children." Why? Because what we behold, we will imitate. In other words, the lifestyle choices of prophetic people are a direct reflection of their revelation of who God is.

The prayer that Jesus prayed in Matthew 6:9-15 has completely changed much of the current church culture. *"On earth as it is in heaven"* has become an affectionate tag line for much of the charismatic/Pentecostal movement. While I exceedingly rejoice in this pursuit to see heaven invade earth as revealed in   Matthew 6:10, I wonder why verse 9 is never included with verse 10, and for the large part, completely ignored by many?

In verse 9, Jesus begins to pray and says, *"Our Father who art in heaven, Hallowed be Thy name."* Then in verse 10 it says, *"Your kingdom come, your will be done, on earth as it is in heaven."* I firmly believe that verse 10, which has so radically impacted this current generation completely hinges upon verse 9 taking place!

What is Jesus saying when He prays to the Father and says, "Hallowed be Thy name"? A paraphrased translation would be: "God, make your name Holy".

It is only when God makes His name Holy among His people that His kingdom will truly come and His will be done on earth as it is in heaven. We have a generation crying out for the kingdom of God to come, but where are the prophetic voices crying out to God, asking that He would make His name Holy first?

## God's Name is Being Defiled

Is it not strange that Jesus begins teaching the disciples to pray by telling them to ask God to make His name Holy? We might casually or flippantly say, "Well, God is holy. That's like telling a desk to become solid or fire to become hot. Why bother?" The answer lies in the fact that God is the most Holy Reality there is, but still

His Name can be and is being defiled in America.

Ezekiel 36:17-23 addresses this very issue as the word of the Lord came to Ezekiel and he prophesied and said,

*"When they came to the nations where they went, they profaned My holy name, because it was said of them, 'These are the people of the Lord; yet they have come out of His land.' "But I had concern for My holy name, which the house of Israel had profaned among the nations where they went. Therefore, say to the house of Israel, 'Thus says the Lord God, "It is not for your sake, O house of Israel, that I am about to act, but for My holy name, which you have profaned among the nations where you went. And I will vindicate the holiness of My great name*

*which has been profaned among the nations,*

*which you have profaned in their midst.*

*Then the nations will know that I am the*

*Lord when I prove Myself holy among you in*

*their sight.'"*

## God is Jealous For His Name

It is absolute foolishness and unbiblical to believe that God is not concerned about His name and how it is being distorted by numerous prophets and teachers in the earth. Why is God so concerned about His reputation and how people see Him? Once again, because it directly affects the way people live! A distorted revelation and interpretation of who God is among the prophetic movement in the earth is directly poisoning the word of the Lord in America.

The new prophetic generation being birthed in the

earth is going to cry out for God to make His name Holy once again. These messengers are going to give their lives to seeing His name restored because they understand that it is the secret to holy and righteous living. When we behold a Holy and Righteous Father, we order our lives accordingly.

## Encounters Like Isaiah

No one can make God's name Holy except God. In asking God to make His name holy, we are asking Him to do something only He can do. Why then did Jesus ask us to pray in this way? I believe it is because when God makes His name holy, there is only one right response from a generation, namely, to therefore live and be holy.

In Isaiah 6, Isaiah describes an incredible encounter where he see's the Lord sitting upon the throne and the train of His robe filling the temple. In verse 3 he says the

Seraphim cry out to one another and say, *"Holy, Holy, Holy is the LORD of hosts, the whole earth is full of His glory."* The temple shook and Isaiah cried out and said, *"Woe is me, for I am ruined! Because I am a man of unclean lips and I live among a people of unclean lips; for my eyes have seen the King, the LORD of hosts."*

The new prophetic generation is going to be marked with encounters like Isaiah. They will be the burning one's released to the American Church who will cry out to God, asking Him to make His name Holy, and when He does, it will release encounters with the holiness of God like no other generation has experienced in history. I believe God is about to redeem His name in America like never before and He is going to do it through the new prophetic generation that embraces every aspect of His Character and Nature.

Mark my words, the kingdom of God will never

become fully manifested in America unless we begin to
cry out for Him to come and make His Name Holy once
again. Jesus Christ fully understood this and that is why
He taught His disciples to pray in Matthew 6 and why He
referred to the Father in John 17 as *"Holy Father"* and
*"Righteous Father"* (17:11; 17:25).

## Irrevocable Calls May Be Deceiving

One of the most confusing elements of the prophetic
movement of the past is how prophets could still
prophesy accurately and perform signs and wonders, yet
be living in a compromised lifestyle. In Romans 11:29
Paul writes, *"...for the gifts and calling of God are
irrevocable."* Another translation says that they are
"without repentance." In other words, individuals can
continue to perform miracles and prophesy without God
revoking or changing His mind, without repenting about

the gifts and calling. The gifts and calling of God are about God and His Graciousness. They have nothing to do with us, or our character. How one handles and operates in the gifts and calling of God is all about one's character. While God may give His gifts and calling "irrevocably," "without changing His mind," and "without repentance," we cannot properly handle and operate in those gifts and calling without repentance!

While prophets (and all others) may be allowed to operate in their gifts and calling without repentance, and only God knows why He allows this, they cannot walk in the fresh anointing of the Holy Spirit without repentance. One does not need to look any further than the life of King Saul who lost the fresh anointing of the Holy Spirit (1 Samuel 15:26), but still prophesied, and then led Israel for another 20 years. It's interesting to note that the only person in the whole nation of Israel who knew and recognized that Saul had lost the fresh anointing of the Holy Spirit was Samuel, the prophet. An entire nation was deceived and led astray by the horrible character of Saul, while the irrevocable gifts and calling upon King Saul's life remained. And so it is today, thousands are being led astray by compromised lives and voices astounding people with their gifts and calling. But these do not have the approval and fresh touch of God upon their lives. They will be like those in Matthew 7, where Jesus said, *"Many will say to Me on that day, 'Lord, Lord, did we not cast out demons, and in your name perform miracles?' And then I will declare to them, 'I never knew you; depart from me, you who practice lawlessness.'"*

## The Need to Distinguish Spirits

The new prophetic generation rising up in the earth will carry great wisdom and discernment to know the difference between the genuine and fresh anointing of God versus prophets that are just operating in irrevocable gifts and callings. As previously stated in an earlier chapter, this is why it is so dangerous to rely upon gifting. Remember, when we stand before Jesus on Judgment Day, He will reward no one for the gifts He gave them. No one with the gift of prophecy will be rewarded for prophesying and no one who was given the gift of miracles will be rewarded for the miracles they performed. We will simply be rewarded for how we stewarded the gifts that we were given.

After Todd Bentley's moral failure during the "Lakeland Outpouring" and the massive fallout in the body of Christ that took place after it, Dutch Sheets, a well known leader and author in the body of Christ, offered a letter of apology to the public. His words are sobering, revealing, and should be received as a fatherly warning to the new prophetic generation.

Dutch wrote and said:

> We, the leaders of the charismatic community, have operated in an extremely low level of discernment. Frankly, we often don't even try to discern. We assume a person's credibility based on gifts, charisma, the size of their ministry or church, whether they can prophesy or work a miracle, etc. (Miracles and signs are intended to validate God and His message, not the messenger; sometimes they validate the assignment of an individual, but never the

person's character, lifestyle or spiritual maturity.) We leaders in the Church have become no different than the world around us in our standards for measuring success and greatness. This has contributed to the body of Christ giving millions of dollars to undeserving individuals; it has allowed people living in sin to become influential leaders – even to lead movements, allowing them influence all the way to the White House.

Through our lack of discernment we built their stages and gave them their platforms. We have been gullible beyond words -- gullible leaders producing gullible sheep. When a spiritual leader we're connected with violates trust, is exposed for immorality or falls below other accepted standards of behavior, it does not exonerate us simply to say we don't condone such behavior. Those we lead trust us to let them know whom to trust. We have failed them miserably in this regard. For this lack of discernment, and for employing and passing on inappropriate standards of judgment, I repent to the Lord and ask forgiveness of the body of Christ.[1]

## Wounds From the Past

The new prophetic generation will not only embrace every aspect of God's Character and Nature regardless of their personal experience, but they will also give the Spirit of God access to every area of their personal life that needs healing and deliverance. As prophetic people, it is not enough to acknowledge the Character and Nature of God. We must allow it to change us inwardly. The Glory of God passed **before and through** Moses on Mt. Sinai, and transformed his face so that it shone. However, it is the desire of God that the new prophetic generation of the New Covenant would not settle for the Glory to pass in front of them and through them, and merely transform them outwardly. The Father wants His Glory – His Character and Nature – to utterly transform us inwardly, so that our inward person reflects His Glory, and then comes out of us in all we say and do.

Several years ago I received a call from a pastor that was struggling with a prophet in his church. While this prophet had become a trusted voice in the community over many years, he began to say some things to the pastor that were alarming. The pastor called me and said, "Jeremiah, this prophet is accusing many women in our community of operating in a Jezebel spirit. Every woman

I give authority to, he brings an accusation to me in private and I need your help."

I agreed to meet with this prophet on behalf of the pastor and as we sat down, I immediately felt prompted by the Spirit to ask him to describe his family growing up, and specifically the relationship that his Mom and Dad had. As I have seen over many years dealing with prophetic people, this prophet immediately put his walls up and had no interest in talking about his past. He tried to change the subject and wanted to talk about what God was saying over the American Church. Refusing to be distracted, I asked the question again. He looked at me right in the eyes and said, "Okay, I hate my Mom and my parents had a terrible relationship growing up." Now we were getting somewhere.

I asked the next question, "How many times have you been married?" He said, "Three, why?" I said, "So you hate women and the reason why you think every woman that get's put in authority is operating in a Jezebel spirit is because you are jealous and still have never dealt with your hatred toward females." The prophet looked at me and said, "How do you know that?" I said, "Because I have sat with thousands of prophetic people just like you who have major character issues and unresolved conflict and they're deceived into believing that all these things will not distort and defile the word of the Lord. And I'm telling you right now that, you need to repent to your pastor, repent to the Lord, and submit to some serious healing before you think about prophesying again. You are releasing poison to the body of Christ rather than healing." After our meeting, the pastor never heard from the prophet again.

While this story is incredibly sad, I have seen it repeated more times than I care to mention. In fact, a majority of pastors that I run into across the country do not trust or have honor in their heart toward the prophetic ministry because they have had interaction with a prophet or prophetic person that carried the word of the Lord, but did not have the heart of the Father because they refused character transformation over the years. Perhaps the most dangerous and blinding position to be in as a prophetic person is to have the ability to hear from the Lord for everyone, except for yourself! It's amazing how many prophetic people are quick to point out the flaws and sins of others, but cannot see their own.

## Issues With Authority

Another primary area of character transformation that the new prophetic generation will give themselves to is walking in healthy relationship with those in positions of authority.

There are too many prophetic people in the earth who have little to no connection with church leadership. They carry deep wounds of rejection, bitterness, unforgiveness, and resentment. These individuals constantly seek to minister prophetically to others despite their pain and it's even more exposed when they minister to those in authority.

Not every church leader is a King Saul of the Old Testament or a religious Pharisee of the New Testament. I'm convinced that many prophetic people who are constantly complaining that the Holy Spirit is not moving in their local assembly need to have their motives checked. The spirit of Jezebel wants freedom in the church so that she can move, but the spirit of Elijah wants freedom in the church so that God can move. I'm concerned that what a majority of prophetic people want right now in the earth is a free for all where they are in charge rather than freedom in the church where the Holy Spirit can move under the facilitation of a shepherd who is called to guard the flock. I repeat: freedom does not equal a free for all where anything goes. These type of environments and atmospheres are what is doing so much damage to the prophetic movement in the earth.

## The Street Prophetess

Several years ago, there was a woman who was traveling from city to city around Florida, claiming to be a prophetess of the Lord. She would enter into churches and begin rebuking the leadership publicly for their sin.

I remember the day she visited the church that I shepherd because I felt her demonic presence in the room. As I kept an eye on her in the back, I specifically asked the Holy Spirit to keep her quiet until after the service. I could tell that no one in the room knew who she was except for me.

As I made my way out to my vehicle after service, sure enough, she was standing right beside it. I walked right up to her and she began cursing me. In fact, she accused me until she was out of breath and had nothing else to say. During her rampage, I began asking the Holy Spirit what was wrong with this woman. Why was she so heavily gifted in the prophetic, yet incredibly unstable and angry toward church leadership? Didn't she know I was prophetic too?

The Holy Spirit said to me, "Jeremiah, her bitterness and unforgiveness toward those who have attempted to hold her accountable regarding her character issues over the years is demonically tormenting her. She is carrying an elitist mentality where she will not submit to the

Godly authority that I have placed in her life because she believes she hears from Me more clearly than anyone else. She has become an island unto herself, measuring herself by herself, and I say to you that she is without understanding. (2 Corinthians 10:12)

**Healthy and Whole**

If the new prophetic generation will give themselves to every aspect of God's character and nature and commit to a life long journey of dealing with their character flaws, they will be like no other prophetic generation that the earth has ever seen.

In fact the new prophetic generation will contend for voices being raised up in the earth that will not tear down with their character what they have built with their gifting. Humility, meekness, and gentleness will be hallmarks of their lives. To the degree that the new prophetic generation allows God's Character and Nature to be worked **in** them, to that degree it will flow **through** them. Releasing individuals who do not know who God is and who do not value inward character transformation to prophesy over people is absolute foolishness. There will be much more to come on this subject in chapter seven. Keep reading!

# - 5 -

# VOICES OF PROPHETIC INTERCESSION

There is a new prophetic generation led by a new breed of prophets coming forth in the earth that will be trained and raised up in the context of night and day prayer. This new prophetic generation has been convinced that their greatest privilege in life is to minister and make intercession to the Lord. They have caught hold of their *"heavenly calling"* as Hebrews 3:1 states, and place more emphasis on the secret place than the public place. These prophetic voices will be more familiar with a prayer room than a playroom. These men and women would rather minister to an audience of One than an audience of hundreds or even thousands. One of the distinct markings of the new prophetic generation will be that they would rather pray to their Father in heaven, than prophesy to their brother and sister on earth. This new prophetic generation craves the attention of the throne room more than the praise afforded to them on a platform and is the very generation Jeremiah spoke of in Jeremiah 27:18 when he said, *"But if they are true prophets and if the word of the Lord is really spoken by them, let them now make intercession to the LORD of hosts…"*

There are prophetic voices that carry the word of the Lord, and then there are prophetic voices that carry "the burden" of the word of the Lord. This new breed of prophets leading a new prophetic generation are actually going to live in a place inside the Father's heart called the, "birthing room." Travail will be their bread and water during the day and the groans of the Father's heart will be what keeps them up at night. They will enter into cities and regions carrying aspects of God's character and nature that are simply not available to others that have not made the secret place a priority. This new prophetic generation understands that cities and regions can be won in travail and intercession down on their knees before they even arrive and prophesy on their feet! Intense seasons of prayer and fasting will precede the arrival of this new prophetic generation. They will carry the fresh fire and word of the Lord wherever they go because they have spent time gazing upon the throne room and receiving the Father's desires in intercession. They will not prophesy from mere impressions, but from being impregnated with the very mind and heart of God. Perhaps the greatest reward of these travailing prophetic voices of intercession will be an accurate assessment of the Father's heart that they will gain through wrestling with Him through prayer and fasting. These messengers understand that it is not enough to deliver the word of the Lord, but rather delivering the word with the Father's heart is what is most needed in this hour.

This new breed of prophets leading the new prophetic generation will travail as Paul travailed in Galatians 4:19 as he said, *"My children, with whom I am again in labor until Christ is formed in you..."* They will not just flippantly or spontaneously prophesy over individuals, churches, and nations as others do, but they will travail in intercession and deep groaning, indescribable by man for days, weeks, months, or years before they ever even speak one word. This new prophetic generation will stand before regions and nations trembling, full of awe and wonder, at God's character and nature that He is longing to share with His people. The new prophetic generation's cry for the body of Christ is simple: Character transformation! It's what they live for! The focus is not on how high you can puff up the saints of God with His words, but how deeply you can connect them with His heart!

## The Wilderness

The travailing intercession and laboring spirit that God wants to place upon this new prophetic generation can only take place in the wilderness where self-serving agendas die and God-breathed strategy and transformation come alive! The cry of this new prophetic generation from the wilderness will be Ephesians 1:17, *"that the God of our Lord Jesus Christ, the Father of the Glory, may give us a spirit of wisdom and revelation in the knowledge of Him."* Carrying a spirit of wisdom and revelation into the character and nature of God is going to be the vision of this new prophetic generation. Just like the four living creatures that stand continually before the throne, these messengers will long to see and behold the beauty of Jesus. They will be Psalm 145 prophets, voices who are eager to declare the memory of God's abundant goodness and shout joyfully of His righteousness. They will declare that, *"The Lord is gracious and merciful; slow to anger and great in lovingkindness. The Lord is good to all, and His mercies are over all his works"* (Psalm 145:7-9). This new breed of prophetic generation will carry inside of their DNA a Psalm 27:4 mandate as it says, *"One thing I have asked from the Lord, that I shall seek: That I may dwell in the house of the Lord all the days of my life, to behold the beauty of the Lord, and to inquire in His temple."*

## The Nasharites

On May 5th, 2014, I had a dream where I found myself in a medieval-looking city with thousands of people who were fearful and oppressed, as the enemy had laid siege to their city. I began to rally them together and tell them that they must fight and not flee. As I gave them instructions, Corey Russell and Allen Hood from the International House of Prayer in Kansas City entered the city. Corey began shouting commands to the people to put on their armor and get ready for battle.

As he finished preparing the people, I began to prophesy to him and say, "Corey! For every 1 voice of awakening that God is releasing in America, He is releasing 7 voices of intercession that will prepare the way for the coming revival." As I said this statement, everything in the dream stopped and I had the captive audience of an entire city. Again I prophesied and said, "Corey! For every 1 voice of awakening that God is releasing in America, He is releasing 7 voices of intercession that will prepare the way for the coming revival!"

I continued on and said, "God gave Lou Engle the Nazarites in this nation, but He is now giving you the Nasharites in this nation. You will raise up a generation of Nash's, voices of intercession that will outnumber the voices of awakening. My Spirit blows through these young Nasharites like a gust of wind, but you will take them and turn them into houses of prayer. The mark of the Nasharites is that they themselves will be called, 'Houses of Prayer'."

I immediately woke up from the dream with fire all over my body. I said to the Spirit as I sat up in my bed,

"This isn't just a dream for Corey Russell, this is a dream to sound the alarm in America for the raising up of voices of prophetic intercession." I began to weep and say, "God we have placed so much emphasis on 'Voices of Awakening' in this nation, and so little time raising up 'Voices of Prophetic Intercession' that will pave the way for the awakening and revival that is coming."

I have had, on several occasions, visitations by the Holy Spirit where He has spoken to me about revival, outpouring, meetings vs. prayer meetings.

## Daniel Nash

At the beginning of the Second Great Awakening in America, there was a man named Daniel Nash who at age 48, began to give himself totally to prayer for the meetings of revivalist Charles Finney. Nash would enter into towns and cities weeks before Finney would have his awakening meetings and travail in the place of intercession and prayer that God might pour out His Spirit upon the meetings. One story is told that Daniel Nash entered a city and could only find a dark cellar to pray in before the revival meetings came to town. Lying prostrate on the ground and groaning, he began to call upon the name of the Lord and succeeded in pulling heaven down to earth. When Charles Finney would eventually come and have the awakening meetings, Nash would usually not attend, but kept praying in secret for souls and deliverance. It has been said that the Second Great Awakening in America brought in several hundred thousand souls to the Lord.

Upon his death in 1831, Daniel Nash's gravestone read: "DANIEL NASH. Laborer with Finney. Mighty in Prayer. Nov 17, 1775-Dec 20, 1831."

The new prophetic generation rising in the earth is a key part of this army of Nasharites. They are voices of deep prophetic intercession that will shift regions and nations as they release the words and heart of God through prayer. Just as Daniel Nash committed himself to be a voice of prophetic intercession that would give time and resources to the place of travail before Charles Finney, the messenger of awakening would preach, even so God is raising up this new prophetic generation. This Nasharite army in the earth will win heaven's blessing and approval before revival and awakening meetings ever take place in cities and regions. God is calling and commissioning this new prophetic generation in America that will wholly give itself to birthing in the spirit realm what has not yet been manifested in the natural.

## Bowls of Intercession

Several nights later on May 10th, 2014, I had another dream that gave me more clarity and revelation into these voices of prophetic intercession. In the dream, I found myself looking down upon the United States where two large bowls filled with incense representing the prayers of the saints were beginning to tip over America. The Holy Spirit immediately spoke to me and said, "You must tell the pastors in America that it's not when the seats are filled that the kingdom will come, but it's when the bowls are full that the kingdom will come in their midst."

A Bible was opened up to Revelation 8 and I began to read, "And when He broke the seventh seal, there was silence in heaven for about half an hour. And I saw the seven angels who stand before God; and seven trumpets given to them. And another angel came and stood at the altar, holding a golden censer; and much incense was given to him, that he might add it to the prayers of the saints upon the golden altar that was before the throne. And the smoke of the incense with the prayers of the saints went up before God out of the angel's hand. And the angel took the censer; and he filled it with the fire of the altar and threw it to the earth; and there followed peals of thunder and sounds of flashes of lightning and an earthquake."

At this, an angel appeared in the dream and began to tip the bowls over several regions of the United States. The Holy Spirit again said to me, "Remember Jeremiah, it's not when the seats are full in the churches that My kingdom will come, but it's when the bowls are full of intercession that My kingdom will be released upon America."

I see a new breed of prophets leading a new prophetic generation that are voices of prophetic intercession, an army of Nasharites, who will dream and long to fill up and watch God pour out bowls of incense over cities, states, and nations. Fame and glamor will not be their banner, but humility and travail will be the wind in their sail. They will love the place of hiding and care not for their own glory because they will give their lives to see God write his-story. This new prophetic generation, the world has yet to see, but in the heart of the Father, He has always meant them to be.

I See a New Prophetic Generation

# - 6 -
# SIMON THE SORCERERS

I see more of a hunger in the prophetic movement to obtain power than to walk in intimacy. I see more of a desire to live under the anointing than to demonstrate Christ-like character. I see more of an appetite to publicly prophesy over thousands than to privately pray to the Father in heaven. I see more of an obsession to chase after someone else's prophetic mantle than to giving our time to discovering our own unique divine design given by the Father alone. I see more of an urge to chase gold dust, feathers, and angels than to encounter the Person of Jesus Christ. All of these pursuits lead to one terrifying end: The rise of a generation of "Simons the Sorcerers" who are currently operating in illegitimate authority!

167

These individuals carry an appearance of walking in deep relationship with Jesus, but in reality, they are collateral damage to the body of Christ. These men and women are dangerous, their motives are impure, and what they primarily pursue and emphasize causes them to live in continual dysfunction. One of the main reasons the prophetic movement is headed for shipwreck is because we are continuing to honor and give individuals positions of authority that have quit on intimacy. These prophetic individuals consistently tear down with their character what they have built with their gifting.

## The Story of Simon

The account of Simon the Sorcerer is told in Acts 8:9ff. when it says, "Now there was a certain man named Simon, who formerly was practicing magic in the city, and astonishing the people of Samaria, claiming to be great; and they all, from smallest to greatest, were giving attention to him, saying, 'This man is what is called the Great Power of God.' And they were giving him attention because he had for a long time astonished them with his magic arts."

Phillip began preaching the good news of the kingdom in Samaria and many men and women were baptized. Even Simon the Sorcerer himself believed and was baptized and immediately started following Phillip because he was amazed at the miracles taking place. When Peter and John heard that Samaria was receiving the word of God, they came down and began to pray that people might receive the Holy Spirit. Laying hands on the new believers, many of them began to be filled and touched by God.

In verses 8:18-24 it says,

*"Now when Simon saw that the Spirit was bestowed through the laying on of the apostles' hands, he offered them money, saying, 'Give this authority to me as well, so that everyone on whom I lay my hands may receive the Holy Spirit.' But Peter said to him, 'May your silver perish with you, because you thought you could obtain the gift of God with money! You have no part or portion in this matter, for your heart is not right before God. Therefore, repent of this wickedness of yours, and pray the Lord if possible, the intention of your heart may be forgiven you. For I see that you are in the gall of bitterness and in the bondage of iniquity.' But Simon answered and said, 'Pray to the Lord for me yourselves, so that*

*nothing of what you have said may come*

*upon me.'"*

One of the keys to understanding the deception Simon the Sorcerer lived in is to identify for what he hungered. He said to Peter and John, "Give this authority to me as well..." Simon's desire for a position of influence and attention was the driving force behind his request to have the apostles lay hands on him. He was quickly becoming addicted to ministry and it was becoming an idol in his life. When this deadly deception overtakes an individual, destruction is right around the corner. Simon was not interested in deep union with Jesus. He was only interested in the miracle working power of Jesus. All activity in the kingdom of God that is not born out of intimacy is unauthorized by heaven!

Peter and John had not only walked with Jesus, but as the crowds noted in Acts 4:13 as the lame crippled beggar had been healed, "they had been with Jesus." Peter and John had waited in the Upper Room to be filled with power from on high, but Simon the Sorcerer was looking for a quick impartation to launch him into ministry.

Peter responds to Simon's request and says, " May your silver perish with you because you thought you could obtain the gift of God with money!" In other words, Simon wanted authority and power so badly that he was willing to use soulish means to obtain them. Peter continues and says, "You have no part or portion in this matter, for your heart is not right before God. Therefore, repent of this wickedness of yours, and pray the Lord if possible, the intention of your heart may be forgiven you..."

I see thousands of Christian young adults in America who, like Simon the Sorcerer, are hungry for the supernatural and are therefore looking for an impartation, prayer or touch from a well known leader in the body of Christ to launch them into their ministry. Rather than seeking intimacy with Jesus Christ and walking in true legitimate kingdom authority like Peter and John, many, just like Simon, are seeking a drive-thru experience because they are hungry for authority, but aren't willing to obtain it legally through intimacy.

## Empowering Illegitimate Authority

We who are prophets and leaders have placed so much emphasis on activation and impartation in our prophetic and supernatural schools in America, and so little time connecting people to the character and nature of God and what Jesus is really like, that we ourselves have blessed and commissioned a generation of Simons the Sorcerers who are operating in illegitimate authority in the body of Christ. Because intimacy and deep union with Jesus Christ are no longer a focus in the prophetic movement, our horrendous levels of discernment have built stages for these Simons the Sorcerers and given them platforms. We have been incredibly gullible as leaders and therefore produced extremely gullible prophetic people.

Peter told Simon the Sorcerer that his heart was not right before God. I believe Simon's desires for power and authority were not only not pleasing to God, but I believe deep within Simon's heart was an impure motive to have the apostles' hands laid on him: He was full of jealousy!

## The Spirit of Jealousy

We are witnessing a mass production of parrots, echoes, and mimics in the prophetic and supernatural movements in America. Too many prophetic people are forfeiting authenticity and originality for formulas and models, even in the supernatural. A large portion of immature and young prophetic people are worshipping well known names in the body of Christ and are hungry for them to have hands laid on them by these individuals. Simons the Sorcerers are signing up for their conferences, their ministry schools, and their meetings. The motive behind this crazy frenzy is not a love for Jesus, but a jealously of others possessing what we do not carry and a total disregard for the need for deep union with Jesus.

I believe that the fuel behind this rapidly growing movement is the spirit of jealousy cloaked in a desire for impartation and activation. Simon did not want the Holy Spirit and power from a pure heart that can only be found in those that spend time with Jesus. He was jealous of the power and authority that Peter and John walked in out of an insecure and wicked heart.

## Deep Union

The new prophetic generation rising in the earth will walk in legitimate authority because of their deep union with Jesus Christ and central pursuit of His character and nature. They have been trained and raised up by prophetic fathers and mothers who saw and understood early on that God was more interested in changing them than using them. This new prophetic generation is not obsessed by or enamored of another's mantle or gifting, but simply enthralled by the invitation to come sit at the feet of Jesus.

## The Coming Distinction

There is a divine confrontation quickly approaching the prophetic movement. I see a collision between a breed of Simon the Sorcerers who are going to be exposed for the illegitimate authority that they walk in and a new prophetic generation who walk in true kingdom authority birthed out of intimacy. Beware of these Simons the Sorcerers. They are addicted to ministry and crave the power and anointing of God from an impure heart of jealousy and a selfish desire to be famous. Instead of carrying a living and active spirit of revelation, Simon the Sorcerer types have to borrow revelation because they have no prayer life. Simon told Peter and John in verse 24, *"Pray to the Lord for me yourselves, so that nothing of what you have said may come upon me."* The greatest distinction between this breed of Simons the Sorcerers and the new prophetic generation rising in the earth will be deep intimacy with Jesus that can only be birthed through deep intercession and travail. Simons the Sorcerers are looking to get launched into ministry by another's touch, but the new prophetic generation is looking to grow in humility under heaven's touch. This can only be accomplished through prayer, fasting and time in the secret place where private battles are won.

# - 7 -
# LOVERS OF THE BRIDE

I see a radical restoration process being released to the body of Christ by the Father Himself between pastors/shepherds and this new prophetic generation in the days ahead. There will be levels of healing and repentance toward one another that has not been seen in any other generation. A key part of this restoration process is the decisive ending of a group of lone ranger prophets in the body of Christ that have no accountability and do not want to submit to any type of spiritual authority.

One of the distinct markings of this new prophetic generation rising up in the earth is that they are interconnected to the body of Christ, and more specifically, they are connected to a local assembly. In past seasons, prophetic voices would prophesy to the body of Christ as outsiders, like ones banished to places of hiding. But this new prophetic generation shall prophesy to the body/bride of Christ as ones belonging to her.

Even now, God is raising up prophetic shepherds who will put on display His character and nature to the body of Christ. They will not hide part of His character and nature while pointing to another, but with eagerness and enthusiasm will seek to present the God of the Old Testament and the God of the New Testament as one!

The days are coming when shepherds will be relieved to see this new prophetic generation in their midst, rather than terrified. The days are upon us when this new prophetic generation will be delighted to see pastors, rather than annoyed. These two ministries will become united in America in the days ahead like never before.

However and whenever the Father chooses to disclose Himself to His people through these prophetic voices, whether He is desiring to pour out His goodness and kindness or whether He needs to bring adjustment and correction, it will be well received by pastors and leaders because of relationship that has been established in previous seasons.

## From Showdown to Lowdown

In September of 2013, I received a series of dreams about a shift that the Holy Spirit is bringing to the prophetic movement. In the first dream, the Holy Spirit said to me, "The days of the "showdown" prophets are coming to an end. I am raising up a company of prophets that will give their lives to the "lowdown". I said to the Holy Spirit in the dream, "I do not understand what you are talking about. Show me this in the Scriptures."

Immediately my very own Bible was placed in front of me and was open to 1 Kings 18. I began reading in verse four, "For it came about, when Jezebel destroyed the prophets of the Lord, that Obadiah took a hundred prophets and hid them by fifties in a cave, and provided them with bread and water." After I read this verse in the dream, I awoke.

The following night I had another dream and the Holy Spirit again spoke to me and said, "I am releasing Obadiah's prophets in the earth. These prophets will have three distinct features to their calling."

He said, "They will be prophets who give themselves to community. I want to put a stop to wandering prophets. They are not only lonely, but the bitterness and anger in their hearts toward others is destroying the gift that I have given them. I am raising up a new breed of prophetic voices that have been fostered in community.

Even as the prophets that Obadiah hid in the caves had to learn how to live among one another where accountability and checks and balances were a must, so I am releasing this very same thing in the earth right now."

He continued, "The second earmark of these prophetic voices is that they are comfortable in hiding. They do not have a need to be seen and heard. They walk humbly before Me and give their lives to staying out of the spotlight until I release them. Elijah was a showdown prophet, but Obadiah's prophets were lowdown prophets. Many are going to be surprised as these voices who, without reputation or finances, carry My words with greater accuracy and timing than many well-known prophets."

Finally He said to me, "The last thing I want you to know about this new prophetic generation is that they live on bread and water as their sources of life. These prophetic voices will not dine at the table of the world or sit amongst kings. They will work jobs and provide for their families, but they carry the bread of life and water from heaven."

## Accountability

I believe much like the prophets that Obadiah hid in the caves while Elijah lived, so a new breed of prophets leading a new prophetic generation have been kept in hiding while many mainstream prophets have been given center stage in this hour. While these prophetic messengers of the past have had to learn how to operate on their own and oftentimes out of a lonely place because they have been rejected by the body of Christ, this new prophetic generation rising in the earth has been forged in community and will possess a love for the body of Christ that has not been seen in any other generation. This new prophetic generation will be called friends and comrades of pastors and other leaders. They will interact and minister as those who are a part of the body, rather than those who have been cast aside and seen as not needed.

One of the greatest blessings of this new breed of prophets leading a new prophetic generation, these messengers that have been kept in hiding for many years and forged in a community setting, is that they will be healthy and mature! They will have an incredible system of checks and balances around them that will not allow them to get away with character flaws and other issues that must be addressed. They will have real and substantial relationships with others in the local community.

An even greater blessing that this new prophetic generation carries is the fact that because they have chosen to remain hidden for so long, they have no need for recognition and the glory that only God deserves. These "Obadiah's Prophets", this new prophetic generation, will carry a spirit of humility and meekness not yet seen before in the prophetic movement. This new breed of prophets leading this new prophetic generation will see one of their primary roles in the body of Christ in the days ahead as protecting the bride rather than violating her!

## Protecting the Bride

Jesus said in Matthew 19:12, *"For there are eunuchs who have been so from birth, and there are eunuchs who have been made eunuchs by men, and there are eunuchs who have made themselves eunuchs for the sake of the kingdom of heaven. Let the one who is able to receive this receive it."*

It was an Ancient Near Eastern Custom to

surround the royal women with eunuchs so that these slaves and servants would not be tempted to violate or sleep with the women. The castration of the male servants and slaves was seen as a method to protect that which was pure and had been set apart for the throne. Jesus said in Matthew 19:12 that there are those who have made themselves eunuchs for the sake of the kingdom of heaven!

This new prophetic generation being revealed in the earth is going to be like these spiritual eunuchs Jesus spoke of in Matthew 19:12. They will give their ministries to protecting the bride of Christ, rather than repeatedly raping her! There are some so-called "prophets" who are currently violating the bride of Christ. Seemingly, they would rather use her for their own wealth and prosperity than nurture and protect her like she deserves to be treated. Make no mistake here; we are talking about the bride of Christ! Too many prophets are having unauthorized intercourse with the bride when they should be making intercession to the bridegroom! There is a distinct shift coming to the prophetic movement in the days ahead. There will be prophets like Simon the Sorcerer that will continue to violate the bride for their own pleasure and then there will be the new prophetic generation who will be like eunuchs that give their lives to protecting and treasuring her unto the pleasure of Christ.

# - 8 -
# THE DAYS AHEAD

The new prophetic generation must not become distracted on their journey to know and understand the character and nature of God. In these critical days in the body of Christ, there is no greater assignment and invitation being released from the Father above than to behold the beauty of His Son Jesus and inquire of Him in His temple (Psalm 27:4). I see a generation of priestly prophetic voices who will give themselves to unceasing night and day prayer that will be one of the greatest waves of refreshing that pastors and leaders have ever known. A.W. Tozer once asked, "What would it be like if the four living creatures filled American pulpits every Sunday? What would they talk about?" These are the living creatures who have eyes in front and in back and who continually stand before the throne and behold the person of Jesus. I believe they would constantly and consistently testify to what Jesus is really like and care not to speak of much else.

What if a new prophetic generation, like the four living creatures, gave their entire ministries to beholding and giving testimony to Jesus? God the Father is restoring His true seers to His body. The new prophetic generation will commit themselves to the place of travail and intercession as they become impregnated with the very purposes of God. These prophetic voices will actually become friends with pastors and leaders, rather than outcasts. Character transformation and the need for inner healing at the foot of the cross will be core messages for these men and women.

God the Father desires to reveal and disclose every part of His character and nature to the bride through His

Son Jesus, the bridegroom, and He is going to do it through this new prophetic generation. Much of the prophetic words that we are going to see delivered to the bride of Christ in the days ahead by this new prophetic generation will have nothing to do with what God wants to **do** for people and all about who God wants to **be** for people. This new prophetic generation will primarily be used to assist people in who they are becoming in Christ and will themselves be committed to this inward character transformation.

## Desperate Seasons

Just as Moses found himself on top of Mt. Sinai in Exodus 34, crying out to see God's Glory, so the body of Christ, in a most critical hour in history, is crying out and searching for her destiny. God's answer to Moses was a revelation of His Goodness as manifested by His character and nature. It wasn't about what God could **do** for Moses, but who God could and desired to **be** for Moses and the nation of Israel that left its mark on them forever.

God's answer to man's most desperate seasons and questions is always an invitation to know Him more intimately. It was the premier longing in the heart of Paul, an apostle, at the end of his days as he said, *"That I might know Him."* I believe what America and Washington D.C. really need is not more prophetic words trying to connect them to their future, but an emergence of a new prophetic generation that will connect them to the God of the future!

**A Vision of God**

I'm convinced that the greatest need of the hour in the prophetic movement is a vision of God that extends way past our own personal experiences regardless of what they might be. We must have a new prophetic generation who will continually stand in the council of the Lord and refuse to drink from the polluted wells of fame, fortune, and personal gain that so many are being seduced by. The prophetic movement must heed the words of Paul to the Corinthians as he said, *"But I am afraid that just as Eve was deceived by the serpent's cunning, your minds may somehow be led astray from your sincere and pure devotion to Christ."*

## Full Quivers

Our quivers must be full of every aspect of God's character and nature so that we might rightly represent Him to the body of Christ. The prophetic ministry must not be seen as "getting words for people" any longer, but rather the source of prophetic ministry must come from, "who does God want to be for this person." The access point into prophesying over individuals, ministries, and nations is the heart of the Father. The new prophetic generation is going to read the heart of the Father back to people, rather than reading people's hearts back to them. As prophetic voices, we must search our hearts and ask ourselves, "What aspects of God's character and nature have I not allowed Him to impart to my life and therefore I'm incapable to imparting them to those I minister to?" Many prophetic voices who love the goodness and kindness of God must learn how to embrace His truth and justness. Other prophetic voices who can only relate to God as a disciplinarian need a revelation of His graciousness and compassion. As the new prophetic generation, we must and will embrace every aspect of who God is in order to rightly represent Him to His people and fully mature in our own unique calling.

## The Enemy of the New Prophetic Generation

Make no mistake about this; the enemy of the new prophetic generation will be a generation of Simons the Sorcerers. There is a divine confrontation being set up in the prophetic movement that will be a collision of that which is counterfeit and soulish and that which is pure and born of the Holy Spirit. The more prophetic and supernatural schools place unnecessary emphasis on impartation and activation without the need for a prayer life, revelation of who God is, and working on character issues, the greater the conflict will be. What will separate the new prophetic generation from the rise of Simon the Sorcerer's will be the Jeremiah 23 reality as revealed in scriptures. The new prophetic generation will walk in legitimate authority because they have won heaven's approval in the place of travail and intercession.

Be on the lookout for the restoration and connection between the new prophetic generation and shepherds and leaders in the body of Christ. This new prophetic generation will be accountable to shepherds and leaders and will give themselves to prayer, fasting, and acts of humility.

The trumpet blast has been clearly released within these pages so that a new breed of prophets leading a new prophetic generation may come forth and be truly recognized in the earth. The call to maturity and putting childish ways behind us in the prophetic movement has never been greater and more necessary.

## The Prophetic Crisis

The prophet Jeremiah commented on the prophetic crisis of his day in Jeremiah 5:31 when he said, *"The prophets prophesy falsely, and the priests rule on their*

*own authority; and my people love it so! But what will*

*you do at the end of it?"*

May we not be so foolish in this hour as to credit the

success of the prophetic ministry in the body of Christ to

how well people love and receive it, especially when it is

not born of the Spirit and comes from the flesh.

As the new prophetic generation, we are not called to

release what people love, but rather what honors and

pleases the Father. In the midst of a generation that loves

and desires prophetic voices who prophesy falsely and

leaders who rule out of their own authority, may a new

prophetic generation rise up in the earth who continually

give themselves to travail and intercession. Let burning

one's who will wholeheartedly embrace every aspect of

the character and nature of God be released into the earth.

I see individuals who are radically committed to inward

character transformation carrying levels of glory and anointing that the body of Christ has never seen before. Prophetic voices are being birthed in the earth right now who know the deep intimacy that produces legitimate authority. These men and women will pursue active

accountability that makes them trusted friends and voices in the body of Christ.

The greatest days of the prophetic movement are upon us! Radical times and seasons require radical demonstrations from above. The new prophetic generation was born for such a time as this and cannot remain ignored, unrecognized, and misunderstood any longer. Their emergence and reception from the body of Christ will be crucial in the days ahead. May we receive and welcome them as good gifts from our Father in heaven. The need and opportunity have never been greater!

# NOTES

1. Dutch Sheets, "Dutch Sheets Apologies for Todd Bentley Lakeland Revival." *The Voice Magazine: Advancing Christian Life & Culture.* The Voice Editor., 22 Aug. 2008. Web.

# ABOUT THE AUTHOR

Jeremiah Johnson received his God given name through a prophetic dream his mother had while he was in her womb. God said that he would be a prophetic messenger and dreamer to the nations, but great complications would mark his birth. Months later, Jeremiah was delivered dead in the delivery room with the umbilical cord wrapped around his neck. However, God intervened and the medical team was able to save both Jeremiah and his mother's life.

Jeremiah was raised in a Charismatic environment where his father pastored a church outside of Indianapolis, IN for nearly 15 years. From the time he was 7 years old, Jeremiah began receiving regular prophetic encounters from dreams and visions at night, to sharing the word of the Lord as he matured in age. God pouring out His Spirit through miracles, prophecy, signs and wonders, and the five fold ministry were all part of the foundation and heritage that Jeremiah was privileged to be raised in as a child and youth.

Jeremiah graduated from Southeastern University in Lakeland, FL where he earned his bachelors degree in Church Ministries. He entered full time ministry at the age of 20 and has had the privilege of traveling and preaching the Gospel of Jesus Christ and prophesying in more than 15 foreign countries and 35 states.

In 2010, Jeremiah planted Heart of the Father Ministry in Lakeland, FL and currently serves on the Eldership Team full time. This community of believers has grown into a gathering of more than 350 saints hungry for revival, prayer, and a mighty harvest of souls. Along with pastoring and being one of the Elders at this growing church plant, Jeremiah also travels and ministers prophetically to leaders and churches all over the United States and abroad. He carries a prophetic message of encountering Jesus Christ and living a consecrated life unto God in more than 35 churches and conferences a year under his traveling ministry, "Jeremiah Johnson Ministries".

Jeremiah loves revival history and has a passion to see a Third Great Awakening sweep through America through a message of repentance, holiness, and the outpouring of the Holy Spirit. He loves to train and equip prophetic people and prophets in their gifting and teach them how to be an asset and blessing to the body of Christ, not collateral damage. He has authored several books on prophetic ministry and is currently working on several more projects.

Jeremiah is married to his beautiful wife Morgan and they have three children: Bella Grace, Israel David, and Lydia Joy. In his spare time, Jeremiah enjoys going to the gym, reading books, and eating American food.

For more information about Heart of the Father Ministry, the church Jeremiah planted in Lakeland, FL please visit www.hotfmlakeland.com. You can catch Jeremiah in Lakeland, FL serving and preaching when he is not ministering on the road or visit him at one of the many cities or nations that he ministers in each year.

# Jeremiah's Other Published Books

*-Chronicles of the Unknown Dreamer 2013*
*-The Micaiah Company: A Prophetic Reformation*
*-I See A New Apostolic Generation*

To purchase your copies and other products today, please visit:
www.jeremiahjohnson.tv